Research and Rhetoric

CLEAR Curriculum Units From the University of Virginia
FOR GRADE 5

Research and Rhetoric

LANGUAGE ARTS UNITS FOR GIFTED STUDENTS IN GRADE 5

Tracy C. Missett, Ph.D.,
Amy Price Azano, Ph.D., &
Carolyn M. Callahan, Ph.D.

Routledge
Taylor & Francis Group
NEW YORK AND LONDON

First published in 2016 by Prufrock Press Inc.

Published in 2021 by Routledge
605 Third Avenue, New York, NY 10017
2 Park Square, Milton Park, Abingdon, Oxon OX14 4RN

Routledge is an imprint of the Taylor & Francis Group, an informa business.

Cover and layout design by Raquel Trevino

ISBN: 9781032144405 (hbk)
ISBN: 9781618214713 (pbk)

DOI: 10.4324/9781003237723

Additional resources can be found at
https://www.routledge.com/9781618214713

TABLE OF CONTENTS

ACKNOWLEDGMENTS

Special credit and acknowledgment must go to the many faculty, researchers, and graduate research assistants who played roles in the development of the CLEAR Curriculum Model; the poetry, research, and folktales units that are included in this series; and the assessments that accompany those units. The CLEAR Curriculum Model was the brainchild of Dr. Catherine Brighton and Dr. Holly Hertberg-Davis. Their original conception of the model led to the drafts of the units mentioned above by then graduate research assistants: Jennifer Beasely, Marla Capper, Jane Jarvis, Maureen Murphy, and Mary Beth Samsa-Hes. Further revisions of the folktale unit were made by Mindy Labernz. Dr. Tonya Moon was a contributor to the development of the performance assessments included in the unit. After field tests and initial implementation of the units by the teachers involved in the study of the units, Dr. Kimberly Landrum worked with the team to further refine the units with the authors of this series. Without each one of them this publication would not have been possible.

And, of course, we must acknowledge the work of Dr. Sandra N. Kaplan, Dr. Joseph S. Renzulli, and Dr. Carol A. Tomlinson, whose foundational work in gifted education guided our thinking in conceptualization of the model and in the development of units that would challenge and engage gifted learners.

Part I

Introduction and Using the CLEAR Curriculum Units

Introduction

As researchers at the National Research Center on the Gifted and Talented, we recently completed a 6-year study of the effectiveness of two units based on the CLEAR Curriculum Model. The CLEAR (Challenge Leading to Engagement, Achievement, and Results) Curriculum Model incorporates elements from three widely-used, research-based models in gifted education—differentiation, Depth and Complexity, and the Schoolwide Enrichment Model—by Carol Tomlinson, Sandy Kaplan, and Joseph Renzulli, respectively. The CLEAR Curriculum Model addresses the recognition by leaders in the field that the heart of effective programming for gifted education services lies in the development and the implementation of curricula and instructional strategies that will challenge and enhance learning outcomes for high-ability learners.

The CLEAR Curriculum Model is comprised of five foundational elements:

1. continual formative assessment,
2. clear learning goals,
3. data-driven learning experiences,
4. authentic products, and
5. rich curriculum.

These elements are integrated into a curricular framework that reflects both the language arts Common Core State Standards and the National Association for Gifted Children Pre-K to Grade 12 Gifted Programming Standards. This integration ensures layers of challenge, opportunities for more in-depth study, and the production of authentic work resembling that of professionals within a discipline.

Teachers who participated in our study implemented two language arts units, one in poetry and one in research, in their third-grade gifted classrooms. The poetry unit, "The Magic of Everyday Things," received the 2012 Curriculum Award from the National Association of Gifted Children. As researchers for the study, we visited more than 100 classrooms across the country and interviewed more than 100 teachers who implemented the CLEAR units. We observed their teaching, their interactions with the curriculum, and student engagement. We also analyzed student achievement data, which indicated that the CLEAR Curriculum works! That is, students who were exposed to the units outperformed peers in gifted classrooms who did not have access to the curriculum.

We also listened to our participating teachers throughout the study. These teachers reported not only that students thrived during the poetry and research units but also that they—the teachers—learned a great deal about best practices in the field of gifted education. Teachers shared that for the first time they finally understood how to differentiate instruction for their students. Buzz phrases like "authentic products" and "formative assessments" came to life, providing a unique source of professional development for teachers whose endorsement credentials vary from state to state. Because no other available curriculum integrates the most popular models of gifted instruction in a way that the CLEAR Curriculum does, these teacher reports provide extraordinary testimony.

Finally, we worked with gifted coordinators who shared their frustrations about the loss of personnel and professional development opportunities vital to the livelihoods of their gifted education programs in the context of a tough economic climate that devalues gifted education and the students served in them. We heard their expressed appreciation for the opportunities for professional development embedded within the poetry and research units themselves.

Throughout our research, we fielded countless e-mails and telephone calls from our participating teachers, their principals, and district coordinators and, resoundingly, they asked: *Where can we get more?*

This three-part series answers that question.

CLEAR CURRICULUM UNITS FOR GIFTED STUDENTS (GRADES 3–5)

The CLEAR Curriculum Units for Gifted Students (grades 3–5) offer two units per grade level for a total of six distinct units based on the CLEAR

Curriculum Model. All units put theory into practice and provide teachers with research-based curricula. What's more is that these units are based on a tested model that has been shown to work. For more on their effectiveness, see an article in the *American Educational Research Journal*, in which Callahan, Moon, Oh, Azano, and Hailey (2015) presented the achievement data documenting the success of the poetry (grade 3) and research (grade 5) units for students exposed to them.

WHAT IS INCLUDED?

Each book in the series contains two grade-level appropriate language arts units based on the CLEAR Curriculum Model, including the award-winning and empirically supported poetry and research units. Each unit incorporates best practices from the field of gifted education while promoting critical literacy skills for the gifted student. Although each book can stand alone, the units are also vertically aligned so that a student advancing through all three grades can encounter innovative and challenging language arts lessons that have clear scope and sequence of learning outcomes that extend the Common Core State Standards (CCSS).

Let us tell you more about the CLEAR Curriculum Model.

THE CLEAR CURRICULUM MODEL

The CLEAR Curriculum Model is a synthesis of fundamental and compatible curricular features from (a) the Differentiated Instruction Model (Tomlinson, 1995, 1999), (b) the Schoolwide Enrichment Model (SEM; Renzulli & Reis, 1985, 2001); and (c) the Depth and Complexity Model (Kaplan, 2005). The CLEAR Curriculum Model was developed as part of a Jacob K. Javits research grant authored by Carolyn M. Callahan, Tonya R. Moon, Holly Hertberg-Davis, and Catherine M. Brighton.

The Differentiated Instruction Model (Tomlinson, 1995, 1999) aims to address the diverse learning needs of students across differing ability levels, interests, and learning profiles. Its success is grounded in modifying three key elements of curriculum—content, process, and product—based on variations in student learning characteristics. As such, differentiation is a flexible instructional model for a broad range of students, including those who are gifted, based on the incorporation of a variety of both curricular and instructional arrangements. Several concepts from differentiation, as conceptualized in Tomlinson's model, lie at the heart of the CLEAR Curriculum Model. For example, the use of continual formative assessments supports teachers in differentiating the academic experiences included in the curriculum and aids teachers in acting on their recognition that gifted students learn and express learning in unique and diverse ways. More specifically, the continual formative assessments provide valuable feedback, or data, to teachers about individual student readiness and inform "next steps" instruction for diverse gifted learners. Thus, the data derived from continual formative assessments allow for tailoring of the curriculum to each student.

Differentiation is also evident in the flexible grouping arrangements provided in the CLEAR units. The use of flexible grouping arrangements facilitates matching the pace of learning, matching degree of challenge and interests of students to instructional tasks, and allowing students to create individualized products that reflect their learning (Tomlinson, 1995, 1999). Whole-group, small-group, and independent activities simultaneously build community and foster autonomy.

The SEM (see Renzulli, 1977; Renzulli & Reis, 1985, 2001) represents one of the most important contributions to the field of gifted education, and SEM has been adopted by many school districts across the county. At its core, SEM stresses the creative process and encourages academic experiences that mirror the work of "real-world" professionals. SEM promotes student engagement through the use of three types of enrichment experiences, which include (a) exposure to extensions of traditional content within the context of its use by real-world professionals (Type I learning experiences), (b) development of process skills that are applied to solving real problems (Type II learning experiences), and (c) investigations of topics and/or creation of products that reflect in-depth investigations into solving real problems in areas of student interest and ability (Type III learning experiences). The feature of SEM that is differentiated at the highest tier is student choice of independent topics for investigation, where students can engage in meaningful learning within the context of real problems in a field and create products demonstrating the skills of an expert in that field. The elements of student choice and authentic investigation are evident throughout the CLEAR units.

The underlying principles of the Depth and Complexity Model (Kaplan, 2005) characterize the CLEAR units and contribute to building layers of challenge and meaning for students. Depth and Complexity employs standards-based curriculum as the basis for promoting academic rigor. The model develops advanced levels of understanding by integrating elements of Depth and Complexity. To provide depth, CLEAR units focus on big ideas, language of the discipline, details, and patterns, and then those concepts are coupled with a focus on complexity, including multiple perspectives, interdisciplinary connections, and ethical issues (Kaplan, 2005). The dimension of complexity affords teachers and students multiple opportunities to think deeply about the content and identify associations and relationships that exist within, between, and among areas of study. Accordingly, the CLEAR units are designed to ensure that students recognize that big ideas and principles are rarely simple. Using these elements of the model also allows for the development of critical literacy skills, as students learn how to "read" bias—their own and others.

Based on the compatible theoretical underpinnings of Tomlinson's, Kaplan's, and Renzulli's curriculum models, as well as principles of exemplary curriculum development in general, the units reflect five foundational elements (see Figure 1) evident throughout all of the CLEAR units.

CONTINUAL FORMATIVE ASSESSMENT

The CLEAR units use formative assessments throughout to provide valuable feedback about students to teachers. Formative assessments serve as a guide to planning instruction with student responses to the assessments informing subsequent instruction. Each unit includes both the formative assessment tool as well as thorough instruction on how assessment data from that tool can be used to differentiate lessons. Use of formative assessment in this manner allows teacher flexibility with the curriculum, thus allowing the instruction to meet students where they are in terms of readiness, interests, and learning profiles. Exit cards, journal entries, and multiple choice responses are examples of formative assessments provided to teachers throughout the units. Figure 2 is an example of an exit card used in the fifth-grade research unit.

CLEAR LEARNING GOALS

The units in this series have clear learning goals consistent with the Pre-K to Grade 12 Gifted Programming Standards (National Association for Gifted Children [NAGC], 2010) and the Common Core State Standards (CCSS). For example, in the poetry unit, third-grade students read the poem "The Fish," a poem more advanced than third-grade students are likely to read. Students are asked to determine the central message and explain how it is conveyed through the details in the poem, to distinguish literal from nonliteral language, refer to parts of the poem and describe how each successive part builds on earlier parts, and explain how the poem conveys mood. These components of the poetry unit integrate multiple standards for third grade in the English Language Arts Standards, Reading: Literature strand of the CCSS. However, these standards are applied to more advanced content to address the advanced readiness levels of gifted students. Throughout all units close attention has been paid to basing lessons on both the CCSS and the NAGC standards.

DATA-DRIVEN LEARNING EXPERIENCES

The philosophical principle underlying the CLEAR units is that gifted learners are diverse in their readiness levels and interests and they learn best when their diverse needs are met in the classroom. Consistent with this philosophy,

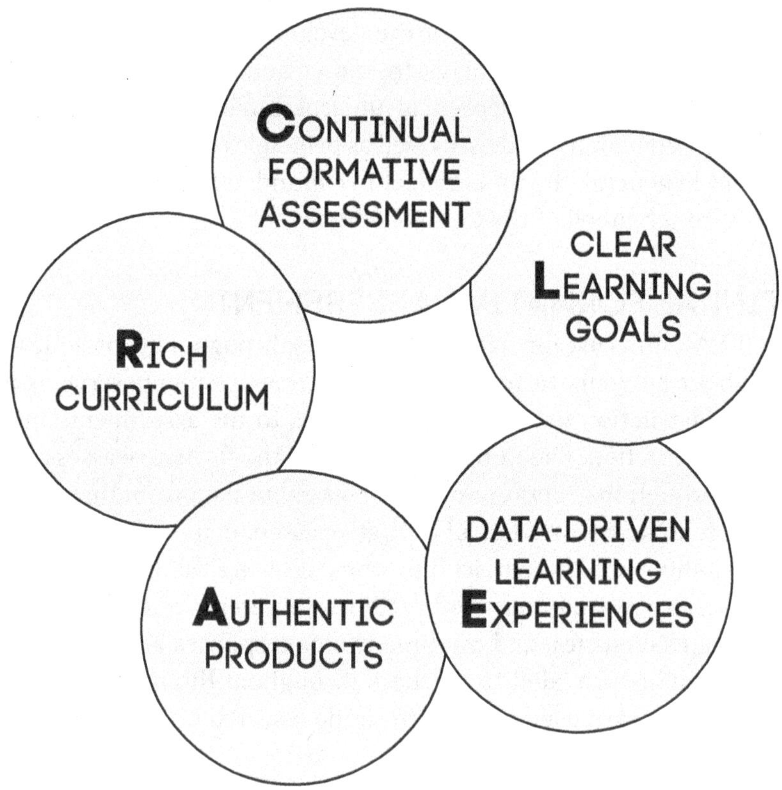

FIGURE 1. THE CLEAR CURRICULUM MODEL.

PREPARATION: FORMATIVE ASSESSMENT 3

In their journals or as an exit card, have students answer one of the first two questions. Have all students answer the third question.

- Before you begin looking for the answers to your research question, what should you do first?
- What is a source?
- How does what you already know about a topic (your prior knowledge) influence how you will go about researching it?

FIGURE 2. SAMPLE "EXIT CARD" FOR FORMATIVE ASSESSMENT.

the units include ongoing formative and summative assessments that provide data for teachers to use in effectively differentiating instruction and learning opportunities for students and assessing student learning.

AUTHENTIC PRODUCTS

In keeping with the Schoolwide Enrichment Model, the CLEAR units provide multiple opportunities for students to create authentic products, to develop real-world skills, and to apply knowledge in relevant contexts. These authentic products take the shape of poetry readings, debates, research presentations, letters to the editor, rhetoric (persuasive arts) journals, and so forth. Students not only acquire knowledge but also use the skills and content they have learned as experts in fields such as poetry, research, and fiction writing.

RICH CURRICULUM

A focus on "big ideas" in the various CLEAR units allows for the achievement of deep understanding. For example, a big idea in the poetry unit is: "Poetry helps readers see the extraordinary (the magic) in the ordinary." A big idea in the research unit is: "Values, experiences, and motivation contribute to the development of an explorer's (reader's) perspective and purpose." In each unit developed using the CLEAR Curriculum Model, students are challenged to question, to investigate, to answer unanswered questions, and then to question what they find! The CLEAR units stress that there are rarely "easy" answers to hard questions—as such, students will sharpen critical literacy skills as they begin to consider varied perspectives and ethical issues within a unit of study.

CRITICAL LITERACY

Literacy skills are no longer limited to the tasks of reading, writing, and speaking. Students are inundated with nonfiction texts and media messages and must have the necessary skills to interpret those messages. Paulo Freire (1970) argued that literacy is always political and redirected the field of literacy instruction to consider social justice and the transformative power of literacy. The CLEAR units will emphasize critical literacy skills, challenging students to consider the political and social implications of the topics and concepts taught. Students are media consumers and must learn to do what Freire (with Macedo, 1987) described as reading the "word" and the "world."

EVIDENCE-BASED PRACTICE

In the current educational environment of accountability, educators, researchers, and policy makers increasingly expect the development and adoption of evidence-based practices, or those that are proven to be effective in raising student achievement. At the same time, a principle contention in the field of gifted education is that gifted students require comprehensive differentiated curricula and instruction to develop their abilities effectively. Thus, the field of gifted education has urged the development and deployment of rigorously conducted curriculum intervention studies to demonstrate that recommended curricula and practices for gifted learners are evidence-based and have demonstrated measurable academic growth for gifted learners.

It was in the context of accountability that the National Research Center on the Gifted and Talented sought to draw from curriculum models with features that had research support and create a new model that could itself demonstrate effectiveness in raising student achievement. As indicated above, the developers of the CLEAR Curriculum Model synthesized components of SEM, differentiation, and Depth and Complexity that were shown to positively impact student learning outcomes.

Specifically, theoretical support for differentiation comes from learning and development theories that propose (a) optimal learning is achieved when learners are exposed to tasks slightly above their current level of performance (Csikszentmihalyi, 1990; Csikszentmihalyi, Rathunde, & Whalen, 1993; Howard, 1994; Jensen, 1998; Sousa & Tomlinson, 2010) and (b) learning should focus on understanding of key knowledge and principles of the field of study rather than rote memorization of information (e.g., Donovan, Bransford, & Pellegrino, 1999; Wenglinsky, 2002). Studies have documented positive effects of the model in student achievement across subject areas, grades, and performance levels and higher level thinking skills with diverse learners in a variety of school settings. Research on the effectiveness of depth and complexity (cited in Kaplan, 2013) has documented academic growth in social studies and language arts among elementary students at all ability levels including gifted students. The effectiveness of SEM has been shown in raising student creative productivity, student personal and social development, and student self-efficacy (e.g., Burns, 1987; Olenchak, 1991; Reis, 1981; Schack, Starko, & Burns, 1991). Moreover, investigations of SEM as a curricular framework in a reading intervention for elementary students of all ability levels including advanced learners have shown higher scores in reading achievement, reading fluency, and students' attitudes toward reading.

The National Research Center on the Gifted and Talented then investigated the effectiveness of the two language arts units—poetry and research—developed from the CLEAR Curriculum Model. After implementing the work in more than 100 classrooms over a period of 4 years, researchers analyzed observations, interviews, teacher logs, surveys, student products, and student outcomes to conclude that students who were provided instruction with the units earned significantly higher achievement test scores than students in classes where the units were not used. A more detailed report of the impact of the units studied can be found in Callahan et al. (2015). Importantly, these positive results were observed in both full-time inclusive gifted settings and pull-out gifted settings. Because the most prevalent service option for gifted learners is pull-out programs with instructional blocks of 45–60 minutes once or twice a week, the units were designed so the whole unit could be completed during the fall/winter or winter/spring sessions in a typical pull-out classroom, including time for ongoing assessments and the creation of an authentic product for each unit. However, the units are structured so that they can also be used daily in self-contained gifted classrooms or with the frequency deemed appropriate by teachers in that setting. Thus, the CLEAR units can be used in a variety of group and classroom arrangements.

OVERVIEW OF THE BOOKS

These books are for gifted education teachers, gifted education coordinators, and regular education teachers who serve gifted students in their classrooms. Each grade-level book offers two complete units of study. Each unit contains 10–20 lessons designed for 45–60 minute classes. Within the units, content and skills are developed to reflect a clear scope and sequence of learning opportunities. The following outline details the organization of the grade-level units based on the CLEAR Curriculum Model and identifies the relevant Common Core State Standards in English Language Arts addressed and extended in each unit.

GRADE 3 UNITS: POETRY AND FAIRY TALES

LITERACY AND CRITICAL LITERACY SKILLS IN GRADE 3 UNITS

(CCSS.ELA-Literacy.RL.3.1–3.10; CCSS.ELA-Literacy.W 3.3–3.6, 3.10)

- All texts/sources are influenced by author's purpose and perspective
- Information comes from multiple sources
- Understanding bias and cultural contexts
- Informed consumers of information

POETRY

In this unit, students will read and analyze various forms of poetry, and write their own poetry anthology. They will learn how to identify and use figurative language to create concrete images from abstract ideas.

FAIRY TALES

In this unit, students will study fairy tales and folklore to understand how and why societal norms and mores are culturally transmitted.

GRADE 4 UNITS: FICTION AND NONFICTION

LITERACY AND CRITICAL LITERACY SKILLS IN GRADE 4 UNITS

(CCSS.ELA-Literacy.RL.4.1–4.10; CCSS.ELA-Literacy.W 4.1–4.10)

- Understanding texts as reflections of culture (politics)
- Understanding informative/explanatory texts contain personal opinions and points of view
- Authors manipulate details
- Readers have filters for information (implicit bias)
- Fiction and nonfiction are equally biased/loaded

FICTION

In this unit, students will read and analyze short stories, develop an understanding of how short story writers develop plot and characters in a concise narrative setting without sacrificing compelling storytelling, and write their own short story.

NONFICTION

In comparison to the fiction (short story) unit, students will study nonfiction (and creative nonfiction) texts to examine how writers use many of the same devices to tell nonfiction stories. Students will read a variety of nonfiction texts and will write their own memoir.

GRADE 5 UNITS: RESEARCH AND RHETORIC

LITERACY AND CRITICAL LITERACY SKILLS IN GRADE 5 UNITS

(CCSS.ELA-Literacy.RL.5.1–5.10; CCSS.ELA-Literacy.W 5.1–5.10; CCSS.ELA-Literacy.SL.5.1–5.4; CCSS.ELA-Literacy.RI.5.1–5.10)

- Creating texts for purpose
- Speakers manipulate audiences
- Yielding and wielding bias
- Understanding the speaker's perspective
- Understanding the audience's perspective

RESEARCH

In this unit, students will learn and employ advanced research skills from crafting open-ended research questions to discerning between reliable sources. Using the Big6 research process, created by Michael B. Eisenberg and Robert E. Berkowitz (1987), students will carry out their own research study and present findings at a research gala.

RHETORIC

Students will engage in a study of Aristotle's *Rhetoric* to answer the question: *When do you appeal to one's intellect, emotions, or sense of morality when trying to persuade?* Students will learn to identify and analyze a variety of rhetorical devices to better understand the art of rhetoric.

Using the CLEAR Curriculum Units

In the introduction, we provided an overview of the three foundational models used in the CLEAR Curriculum Model (Differentiated Instruction Model, Schoolwide Enrichment Model, and the Depth and Complexity Model), the five foundational elements of CLEAR (continual formative assessment, clear learning goals, data-driven learning experiences, authentic products, and rich curriculum), evidence from a multiyear research study, and an overview of the units in this curriculum series. In this section, we offer more specific information about the elements you will find in each unit, including information about how the CLEAR Curriculum Model comes to life in the teaching of these language arts units.

THE SCOPE OF EACH UNIT

Each unit emphasizes "big ideas" within a major focus area in language arts instruction: poetry, storytelling, fiction, nonfiction, rhetoric, and research. Consistent with national standards, these big ideas are then delineated by objectives and vocabulary terms For example, a big idea in the poetry unit is for students to see the extraordinary in the ordinary. For students to grasp that abstract notion, they must practice reading and writing many forms of poetry. They need to understand how poets use figurative language to render the abstract concrete or the inanimate animate. And they do this while becoming poets—collecting ideas, reading as writers, workshopping their poems, and publishing their work. These big ideas allow teachers and students to concentrate efforts on the "how" and "why" of literacy instruction.

Each unit begins with an overview of the big ideas, learning objectives, and a unit outline that gives an overview of each particular lesson, the related big idea(s), and the targeted skills. The units also begin with a section on "preparing to teach" which provides teachers with information related to resources, materials, classroom environment, classroom management, and ongoing assessments as they relate to that particular unit.

Instruction in each unit is based on a preassessment that is the lead-off activity. Each unit contains several formative assessments that are integrated throughout, and concludes with performance and summative assessments. In each unit, students will produce an authentic product (collection of poems, short story, memoir, speech, etc.). The units also include rubrics for assessing these authentic products.

THE ICONS USED THROUGHOUT THE UNITS

Integrated throughout the lesson plans are a series of icons or symbols intended to draw your attention to the particular content focus, learning objective, or instructional configuration of each learning activity. Some of these icons are derived from Sandra Kaplan's Depth and Complexity Model, while others have been developed specifically for the CLEAR Curriculum Model used in these units. Icons fall into five major categories: Lesson Organization, Literacy Focus, Differentiation, Discipline Exploration, and Subject Analysis. These icons serve as a "quick glance" roadmap to guide instruction. Here we will explain the icons and how they are used throughout the units.

LESSON ORGANIZATION

There are four icons used to indicate how students should be grouped for instructional activities.

Whole-Class Instruction. The teacher leads an activity with the entire class together.

Small-Group Work. Students engage in a learning task in pairs or small groups of 3–5.

Independent Work. Students work on their own in identifying a topic of study, conducting research, and writing or using other modes of expression to present information or demonstrate understanding.

Anchor Activity. As students work at different paces, there will be times when some students finish a task sooner than others. An anchor activity is a task on which students work (usually independently) after they complete other class work. An anchor activity is meaningfully related to the learning objectives of the lesson or unit, allowing students to explore essential ideas, rather than simply a time-filler. All students will have a chance to work on anchor activities over the course of a unit.

LITERACY FOCUS

There are four icons used to indicate the literacy focus of instruction.

Word Study. Students are engaged in learning and practicing how to decode words by breaking them down into their component parts such as sounds, syllables, roots, prefixes, and suffixes. Each student works with words that match his or her own readiness level.

Reading Comprehension. Students are reading for the purpose of understanding and practicing comprehension strategies.

Writing. Students are engaged in one or more stages of the writing process.

Critical Literacy. Students are engaged in thinking about the political and/or social implications of the topics and concepts being taught. They are reading the "word" (text) and the "world" (context).

DIFFERENTIATION

There are four icons to indicate how teachers can differentiate a particular activity.

Differentiation by Readiness. Readiness-based differentiation is the process of adjusting learning experiences to match individual students' levels of past achievement and point of development. Readiness refers to what students already know, understand, and can do related to the learning objectives for a particular task, lesson, or unit. A student's level of readiness might vary depending on his or her background knowledge, prior learning experiences, and profile of competencies related to different topics or kinds of activities. When learning tasks are matched to a student's level of readiness (i.e., within the student's zone

of proximal development), the student has the opportunity to work at something that is both challenging and rewarding. When a task is too challenging or not challenging enough for a student, learning is unlikely to occur. Thus, it is essential that general lesson plans be adjusted to better tend to differing levels of readiness among students. Students might work in readiness groups or independently on tasks that are differentiated by readiness.

Differentiation by Interest. Interest-based differentiation refers to the process of adjusting learning experiences to match individual students' interests. When students have the opportunity to work in an area of personal interest to them, they are more likely to become motivated to learn and therefore actively engaged in the learning process. Teachers can attend to students' interests by offering a choice of several materials or topics, by inviting students to suggest their own topics for study, or by allowing students to sometimes work in interest-based groups.

Learning Profile. Learning-profile-based differentiation is the process of adjusting learning experiences to match an individual student's pattern of strengths, weaknesses, and preferences that determines how he or she takes in, makes sense of, and expresses information. Learning profile is shaped by factors such as culture, gender, and learning style preferences. Teachers can provide opportunities for students to work in ways that match their learning profile preferences by incorporating multiple modes of expression and ways of working into the life of the classroom.

Twice-Exceptional Learners. Some students in gifted classrooms also have a disability—such as a specific learning disability, Attention Deficit/Hyperactivity Disorder, autism spectrum disorder, and/or an emotional and behavioral disorder—that impedes their ability to learn. These students are commonly referred to as twice-exceptional or "2E" learners. As more students with disabilities are participating in gifted programs, it is important to shift the primary focus of instructional strategies away from remediation and social skills improvement for gifted students with disabilities and toward their strengths, talents, and interests to promote social, emotional, and academic gains, and also to expose these students to rich curricula. The CLEAR language arts units provide a structured model with instructional strategies directed toward developing student strengths (e.g., ability grouping, acceleration, formative assessment) that are recommended for both gifted students and students with disabilities. However, in recognition that these students will sometimes need additional support structures, the 2E icon supports teachers in their use of effective instructional strategies for twice-exceptional students.

DISCIPLINE EXPLORATION

There are five icons used to explain how the discipline can be explored and where the teacher can focus student attention during instructional activities.

Big Idea. A big idea refers to an essential understanding about a topic or discipline that students should take away from the lesson or unit. It often helps to "unpack" or explain an important concept or the relationship between two or more concepts. Big ideas help students move beyond the facts and skills they are learning to focus on what is fundamentally important, enduring, and transferable about the topic. For example, in the poetry unit, students explore the big idea that poetry helps readers see the extraordinary in the ordinary. This is a big idea that guides the work of contemporary poets as they use concrete, sensory language and specific imagery to add layers of meaning to the description of everyday objects, events, and experiences. The big idea can be explored across different poems, poets, and periods of history. In this way, the big idea is a focal point that holds the unit together; students are gradually guided, through a range of learning activities, to arrive at a deep understanding of the big idea. The term *big idea* is sometimes used synonymously with principle, generalization, or understanding.

Place-Based Pedagogy. This task allows students to think critically about how this text (or context) relates to their own sense of place or local community.

Language of the Discipline. The task helps students achieve greater depth of understanding by coming to know and apply the vocabulary of professionals in the academic discipline.

Tools of the Discipline. The task helps students achieve greater depth of understanding by coming to know and apply the ways of thinking and working of professionals in the academic discipline.

Real-World Application. The task requires students to apply the language and tools of the discipline in an environment or activity similar to what an expert in the field would experience.

SUBJECT ANALYSIS

There are three icons used to indicate how a task offers students depth and complexity of a particular topic.

Details. The task helps students achieve greater depth of understanding by studying the essential details relevant to what they are learning.

Patterns. The task helps students achieve greater depth of understanding by analyzing the patterns and trends that can be identified in what they are learning.

Over Time. The task helps students achieve a more complex level of understanding by guiding them to consider what they are learning from a historical perspective.

TIPS

The tip icon indicates an important note for the teacher. The tip might refer to something to watch out for, such as potential classroom management issues or a particular type of talent potential during a learning activity.

ASSESSMENTS IN THE UNITS

There are four types of assessments used throughout the units. Each unit begins with a preassessment to gauge students' initial interest and conceptual knowledge of the unit topic. For example, in poetry students are asked: *What do you know about poetry? What are some of the ways poets make their poems interesting? What would you like to learn about poetry in the next few weeks?* Teachers can use responses to understand students' prior knowledge about the subject and plan subsequent instruction accordingly.

The units also utilize formative assessments throughout. Formative assessments are used to inform next steps in the lesson. Directions are provided on how to use the assessment data to inform instruction in the activities or lessons that follow. For example, in the poetry unit, students take a poetry survey as a formative assessment after Lesson 5. Additionally, teachers are provided with the following instructions for utilizing the data:

> Use information from the assessment to determine whether there is any content you have taught so far that you need to review or reinforce. For example, you might find a group of students having trouble remembering the definition of an adjective or confusing concrete and abstract nouns, and you can plan to take these students aside for a "mini-lesson" at a convenient time. Students' responses to questions about what they would still like to learn might help you choose resources and try to incorporate opportunities to address students' individual interests in later lessons.

Other formative assessments might provide instructions for making decisions about how to group students.

The units also utilize performance and summative assessments. Students will be asked to produce authentic products throughout each of the units, and these final assessments will provide an opportunity for teachers and students to assess learning. For example, the poetry unit ends with a poetry reading and a collection of original works, along with a review of a canonical poem.

GETTING STARTED

The lessons within each unit are clearly marked, along with the assessments, and icons will further direct your instruction. The two units for each grade level can be taught in whichever order you prefer. We hope you and your students enjoy these CLEAR Curriculum units.

Part II

Unit Plans

Unit 1 Exploration and Communication A Researcher's Journey

BACKGROUND

Exploration and Communication is a curriculum unit designed to help students explore a variety of nonfiction texts and expand their skills in research, writing, and the use of reading comprehension strategies. Through this unit, students will develop a sense of themselves as researchers as they focus on the dual concepts of exploration and communication in research.

Using the metaphor of researcher as explorer, students will learn how to channel their interest in an area, person, or topic into a worthwhile research project. Students will set out on a "knowledge expedition" by framing initial research questions, and searching, organizing, and evaluating information from different kinds of texts. Students will explore how multiple perspectives can be brought to a topic and examine how perspective shapes the way we interpret and share information. Using the concept of researcher as communicator, students will learn how to share their findings with a specified audience in clear and meaningful ways, including through writing and speaking.

To structure their research, students will learn and use the Big6 research process. Developed by Michael B. Eisenberg and Robert E. Berkowitz (1987), the Big6 is an information problem-solving model that enables students to search for information and use skills systematically to find, use, apply, and evaluate information in texts for specific tasks (1987).

The activities and assessment products included in this unit are designed to help students develop essential research skills that can be applied across a range of disciplines. Students will have the opportunity to work with materials and ideas that suit their individual interests and need for challenge. Students should walk away with an understanding that research is an organized and systematic way of finding answers to important questions. By the end of the unit, each student will have designed and conducted a complete research project, which they will share with an audience of students, parents, and teachers at a classroom Research Gala.

OBJECTIVES/STANDARDS

This unit is designed to be consistent with common state fifth-grade reading and writing standards, and national standards outlined by the National Council of Teachers of English (NCTE; National Council of Teachers of English & International Reading Association, 2012). It also aligns to the fifth-grade Common Core State Standards (CCSS; an alignment chart is provided on p. 265). This unit addresses the following objectives:

STUDENTS WILL KNOW THE FOLLOWING TERMS

- *Research* is a detailed study of a subject, especially in order to discover (new) information or reach (a new) understanding.
- A *source* is something such as a person or document that supplies information.
- An *expedition* is a journey undertaken by a group of people with a definite objective.
- *Plagiarism* is using others' ideas and words without clearly acknowledging the source of that information.
- *Synthesis* is the combining of separate elements to form a whole.
- *Paraphrase* is a restatement of a text or passage giving the meaning in another form as for clearness; rewording.

STUDENTS WILL UNDERSTAND THE FOLLOWING BIG IDEAS ABOUT READING AND RESEARCH

- Research is an organized and systematic way of finding answers to questions.
- Readers can use strategies and structure to make meaning from texts.

- Purposes and perspectives influence how readers and writers (explorers) interact with texts.
- Values, experiences, and motivation contribute to the development of an explorer's (reader's) perspective and purpose.
- The contributions of an explorer's journey can be analyzed from various perspectives.

STUDENTS WILL DEMONSTRATE THE FOLLOWING SKILLS

- Apply self-monitoring strategies when reading.
- Evaluate the effectiveness of a text for a particular purpose.
- Compare and contrast similar text features in different sources.
- Read a passage and paraphrase what was read (note-taking system).
- Access prior knowledge when reading.
- Sort and classify texts by genre.
- Determine text features.
- Identify and compare text features in Internet sources and textbooks.
- Determine multiple purposes for section headings in expository texts.
- Clearly define a task.
- Formulate research questions and hypotheses.
- Examine multiple perspectives on a topic.
- Determine incremental benchmarks to reach a goal.
- Identify appropriate resources to answer a research question.
- Use particular strategies to locate sources.
- Access a variety of sources.
- Determine the accuracy and reliability of online sources.
- Critically evaluate the quality of a source.
- Cite evidence in support of opinions.
- Students synthesize multiple sources of information for communication.
- Present a synthesis of various sources.
- Present original research to an audience.
- Determine a set of criteria on which to judge quality research.
- Determine effective methods to communicate research findings.
- Define plagiarism and describe its consequences.
- Evaluate the work of colleagues using established criteria.
- Monitor comprehension of texts (metacognition).
- Work collaboratively in conducting and presenting research.

UNIT 1 OUTLINE

	Big Idea(s)	Overview	Skills
Unit Preassessment			
Lesson 1	≫ Exploration is a metaphor for understanding that research is an organized and systematic way of finding answers to questions.	*Who Are Explorers?* ≫ Consensus building activity. ≫ Anticipation guide for introducing unit content. ≫ Who Am I?: An Exploration.	≫ Cite evidence in support of opinions. ≫ Examine multiple perspectives.
Formative Assessment 1			
Lesson 2	≫ Research is an organized and systematic way of finding answers to questions.	*Concept Exploration* ≫ Explore multiple concepts related to the unit and consider the relationships between concepts. ≫ Think about researchable questions. ≫ Introduce the knowledge expedition.	≫ Synthesize knowledge for communication. ≫ Compare and contrast various concepts. ≫ Formulate hypotheses.
Lesson 3	≫ Purposes and perspectives influence how readers and writers ("explorers") interact with texts. ≫ Readers can use strategies and structure to make meaning from texts. ≫ Research is an organized and systematic way of finding answers to questions.	*Fiction and Nonfiction: What's the Difference?* ≫ Examine and analyze the features of nonfiction texts. ≫ Introduce the Big6.	≫ Sort and classify texts by genre. ≫ Determine text features.
Formative Assessment 2			
Lesson 4	≫ Research is an organized and systematic way of finding answers to questions. ≫ Values, experiences, and motivation contribute to the development of an explorer's (reader's) perspective and purpose.	*What Do I Know and Where Do I Go?* ≫ Examine research topics and explore information seeking strategies. ≫ KWL.	≫ Access prior knowledge through discussion. ≫ Compile a list of research sources.

	Big Idea(s)	Overview	Skills
Formative Assessment 3			
Lesson 5	≫ Readers can use strategies and structures to make meaning from texts. ≫ Research is an organized and systematic way of finding answers to questions.	*Texts on the Internet: Friend or Foe?* ≫ Consider information seeking strategies. ≫ Compare/contrast texts. ≫ Conduct independent web investigation.	≫ Determine multiple purposes for section headings in expository texts. ≫ Create or insert missing section headings in an expository text.
Lesson 6	≫ Research is an organized and systematic way of finding answers to questions. ≫ Purpose and perspectives influence how reader and writers interact with text.	*How to Create a Research Question* ≫ Use an organizational system to focus on topics. ≫ Distinguish between thick and thin questions. ≫ Develop research questions.	≫ Develop research questions.
Lesson 7	≫ Readers can use strategies and structure to make meaning from texts. ≫ Research is an organized and systematic way of finding answers to questions.	*Exploring Texts: Metacognition and Marking* ≫ Learn strategies for taking notes and monitoring reading comprehension using nonfiction texts.	≫ Monitor comprehension (metacognition). ≫ Work cooperatively and independently to apply INSERT strategy. ≫ Locate and access various library materials.
Lesson 8	≫ Research is an organized and systematic way of finding answers.	*A Return Expedition: Working as Researchers* ≫ Locate and evaluate nonfiction texts in the library.	≫ Locate and access various library materials.
Lesson 9	≫ Research is an organized and systematic way of finding answers to questions.	*Working as Researchers: Exploring Texts and Organizing Ideas* ≫ Introduce the concept of plagiarism and discuss and evaluate scenarios involving plagiarism. ≫ Learn to paraphrase passages using a note-taking system.	≫ Define plagiarism and describe its consequences. ≫ Collect and analyze information relevant to topic/question. ≫ Read a passage and paraphrase what was read (note-taking system).

	Big Idea(s)	Overview	Skills
Formative Assessment 4			
Lesson 10	≫ Research is an organized and systematic way of finding answers to questions.	*Working as Researchers: Reexploring Texts and Reorganizing Ideas* ≫ Evaluate progress as researchers and engage in independent research.	≫ Locate and access various library materials. ≫ Identify an area for improvement.
Lesson 11	≫ Research is an organized and systematic way of finding answers to questions.	*Researchers as Project Designers* ≫ Consider different presentation options and design independent research projects.	≫ Determine effective methods to communicate research findings. ≫ Determine incremental benchmarks to reach a goal.
Lesson 12	≫ Research is an organized and systematic way of finding answers to questions.	*Researchers as Presenters* ≫ Collaborate to determine a list of characteristics of and criteria for effective presentations.	≫ Determine a set of criteria on which to judge quality research. ≫ Conduct independent research.
Lesson 13	≫ Research is an organized and systematic way of finding answers to questions.	*Preparation for Gala* ≫ Finalize projects and prepare for the Research Gala.	≫ Synthesize multiple sources of information.
Lesson 14	≫ Research is an organized and systematic way of finding answers to questions.	*Preparation for Gala: The Dress Rehearsal* ≫ Participate in a dress rehearsal for the Research Gala.	≫ Present a synthesis of various sources.
Lesson 15	≫ Research is an organized and systematic way of finding answers to questions. ≫ The contributions of an explorer's journey can be analyzed from various perspectives.	*Research Gala* ≫ Present research projects to peers, parents, and other visitors at a Research Gala.	≫ Present original research to an audience.
Performance Assessment **Summative Assessment**			

PREPARING TO TEACH THE UNIT

RESOURCES AND MATERIALS

The texts used to model reading strategies came from a public domain database called Project Gutenberg (http://www.gutenberg.org).

Extra resources concerning the teacher's exploration into "Who Really Discovered America?" are listed below. Some possible discoverers of America include: Hoei Shin, Brendan the Bold, Bjarni Herjo'lfsson, Prince Madoc of Wales, Leif Ericsson, Christopher Columbus, and Chief Howling Wind of the Cree Nation.

- Exploration of North America: http://www.history.com/topics/exploration/exploration-of-north-america
- The Voyage of Brendan the Navigator: http://www.irishcultureandcustoms.com/ASaints/BrendanNav.html
- Did the Chinese Beat Columbus to America?: http://history.howstuffworks.com/history-vs-myth/chinese-beat-columbus.htm
- Bjarni Herjo'lfsson: https://en.wikipedia.org/wiki/Bjarni_Herjólfsson
- Prince Madoc of Wales: http://www.robertsewell.ca/madoc.html
- Leif Ericsson: http://www.mnc.net/norway/Leif.htm or http://www.viking.no/e/people/leif/e-leiv.htm
- Christopher Columbus: http://www.enchantedlearning.com/explorers/page/c/columbus.shtml

Links to web-based lesson materials are available in each lesson plan and on the book's webpage at http://www.routledge.com/assets/clientpages/Research_Rhetoric.aspx.

CLASSROOM ENVIRONMENT

The teacher is encouraged to set up a classroom environment that is conducive to individual exploration and independent work. Establishing a daily routine and a consistent classroom physical environment is imperative. Here are some very practical tips to help you execute a successful unit:

- Establish "homes" for all kinds of materials—journals, dictionaries, personal library books, etc.
- The teacher in this unit (you!) is exploring a research question such as: Who really discovered America? Prior to the start of the unit, ask the librarian in your school to compile resources pertaining to your chosen topic that you can keep on a cart in your classroom.
- Establish a "home base" where students will do independent work. This most likely will be their desks. When you say "go to home base" all stu-

dents should know where to go and that the activity is a quiet/independent one.

CLASSROOM MANAGEMENT

In order for students to be "exploring" material that is on their reading level and of interest to them, teachers must be flexible. Each student will be working with texts that are of appropriate readability and interest to him or her. This will require the teacher to wear multiple hats and be attuned to the particular needs of each student.

Each student will need to have a research portfolio. A three-ring binder with tabs for each child will be provided. All work pertaining to the research investigation will be kept in this binder (or research portfolio) in a marked area in the classroom. Students should *rarely, if ever,* take their binders home. You will need to routinely check these to monitor each student's progress.

ONGOING ASSESSMENT

The unit preassessment is administered to students prior to the first lesson. The purpose of the preassessment is (1) to assess what students already know about the purpose and structure of nonfiction texts as well as effective research strategies, which will help tailor the activities and group students appropriately, and (2) to provide a baseline for comparison at the end of the unit so that the teacher can assess the growth of each student throughout the course of the unit. A computer- and library-use preassessment is also included to help teachers see which students may need scaffolding in these areas.

Formative assessments are administered to students throughout the unit in order to (1) assess students' developing skills so that resources and activities can be tailored to each student, and (2) assess what students already know about research, which will help tailor the activities and group students appropriately.

There are two summative assessments for this unit. The first is the culminating project ending in the research gala. The students' final products will serve as the evidence of their learning and the provided rubric will serve as the evaluation tool. There will also be a performance task conducted the day after the research gala. All the necessary materials are provided for this assignment.

THE CLEAR CURRICULUM MODEL

This unit has been designed using the CLEAR Curriculum Model. The CLEAR (Challenge Leading to Engagement, Achievement and Results) Curriculum incorporates elements from three research-based curriculum models—differentiation, Depth and Complexity, and the Schoolwide Enrichment

Model—by Carol Tomlinson, Sandy Kaplan, and Joseph Renzulli, respectively. These elements are applied to a curriculum framework that is consistent with state and national standards in reading, but builds layers of challenge and opportunities for more in-depth study authentic to the work of professionals within a discipline, to better meet the needs of all students. Refer to page 15 for more information about the CLEAR Curriculum Model.

ICONS EXPLAINED

Integrated throughout the lesson plans are a series of icons or symbols intended to draw your attention to the particular content focus, learning objective, or instructional configuration of each learning activity. Some of these icons are derived from Sandra Kaplan's Depth and Complexity curriculum model, while others have been developed specifically for the CLEAR Curriculum Model used in these units. Refer to page 16 for an explanation of each icon.

LESSON

1 Who Are Explorers?

MATERIALS

- ✓ Student journals (3-ring binder)
- ✓ Handout 1.1: Unit Preassessment
- ✓ Handout 1.2: Computer/Library Preassessment (optional)
- ✓ Handout 1.3: Anticipation Guide
- ✓ Handout 1.4: Who Am I?: An Exploration

Exploration is a metaphor for understanding that research is an organized and systematic way of finding answers to questions.

OBJECTIVES

Students will:

- ✓ cite evidence in support of opinions, and
- ✓ examine multiple perspectives.

- Consensus

SEQUENCE

UNIT PREASSESSMENT

1. Administer the Unit Preassessment (Handout 1.1). Explain to students that this assessment is not for a grade. Rather, it is to find out how much they already know about exploration. An optional computer- and library-use preassessment is also included (Handout 1.2) if you feel that students may need scaffolding in these areas.

WARM UP

2. Ask students to respond to the following prompt in their journals: *What does it mean to explore? How many explorers can you name? Name as many as you can!* Allow students time to write independently. Afterward, briefly give students a chance to share their responses with the whole group if they choose.

If you have not used journal entries as warm-up or closure activities in the past, explain this routine to the students. Students have "journal" tabs in their binders. Keep binders in a consistent location in the classroom. You will use journal entries to (1) help you determine flexible groups and (2) provide you with data concerning each student's developing grasp of the unit's big ideas.

ACTIVITY: ANTICIPATION GUIDE

3. Distribute Handout 1.3: Anticipation Guide. Explain to students that the first part of this activity will be completed independently. You will guide the students through the task, reading each statement and allowing time for students to respond.

Students are to write an A if they agree with the statement or a D if they disagree with the statement. In the space beneath each statement, have students write at least one sentence explaining why they agree or disagree.

4. When all students have completed the guide, students should work in groups of three to four to reach a consensus about each statement. They all must arrive at the same opinion about each of the statements. Make it clear that at first they may not agree; however, the team should discuss each statement until they reach an agreement. Either they all agree with the statement or they all disagree with it. Ask if there are questions.
5. Walk students through the first statement, prompting groups with questions such as: *Do you all agree with this statement? Do you all disagree?* If students cannot reach a consensus, tell them to talk it through. If students still cannot seem to agree, advise them to skip that "controversial" statement and move on.
6. Instruct students to work through the rest of the guide in their small groups. Move around the room making sure students are on task.

If a group struggles to reach a consensus, challenge them to find a word or two they can change that would allow the group to agree or disagree.

DISCUSSION: WHAT IS EXPLORATION?

7. Lead a whole-group discussion about exploration. Ask: *What is it? How might we define it?* (This class definition will be needed for the next lesson.) Invite students and groups to share/debate their thoughts about the Anticipation Guide statements. Collect Handout 1.3 (You will use these to provide comments to students about this activity and return them to students' research portfolios).

To develop this understanding, have students brainstorm the words *explore*, *exploration*, and *explorer*. Consider making a "thinking" or "concept" map where students can chart their understandings throughout the unit.

If you have not done much student-centered discussion in your class before, you may need to discuss and establish some ground rules. Sample discussion ground rules are listed below. You can revise or adjust these as you see fit.

- Equal participation.
- Eye contact with all.
- Respect others' opinions.
- Build on what the last person said.
- No side conversations.

HOMEWORK

8. Distribute Handout 1.4: Who Am I?: An Exploration and have students complete the assignment for homework.

PREPARATION: FORMATIVE ASSESSMENT 1

9. Close this introductory lesson by having students return to their journals. Ask students to respond to two of the following questions:
   - ✓ Are you an explorer? Why or why not?
   - ✓ Why do explorers explore?
   - ✓ What would you like to explore?

10. Make sure all binders are returned to the specified location.
11. **Using the assessment data:** Use the anticipation guide and journals to evaluate each student's understanding of the concept of exploration.
    - ✓ Do some students seem to know more about exploration than others?
    - ✓ Can some students name a few or several explorers?
    - ✓ Do some students seem to have a greater interest in exploration than others?

HANDOUT 1.1

UNIT PREASSESSMENT

You have been asked to explore answers to a tough question: Who *really* discovered America? You may have your own answer to this question. However, you have been hired by a group of historians to help research and present what more you can learn about who first discovered America. You may find that you've been wrong!

How might you go about answering the question? Create a plan of action in the space provided below. What will you need to do first? Second? Third, and so forth? You may not have any information now, but what's your plan for finding out who *really* discovered America?

HANDOUT 1.2

COMPUTER/LIBRARY PREASSESSMENT

1. Do you have a computer at home?
   a. We don't have one at home.
   b. We have one, but I don't use it.
   c. We have a computer at home, and I use it a lot.

2. Do you know how to get onto the Internet?
   a. Yes
   b. No

   If yes, use the space below to describe how to get onto the Internet.

3. Have you ever used a computer at school?
   a. Yes
   b. No

4. If you wanted to find out about frogs in your school library, how would you go about getting information?

5. In the library, have you ever looked for anything other than a book to take home and read for fun?
   a. Yes
   b. No

6. True or False: Information you find on the Internet is always true.
   a. True
   b. False

HANDOUT 1.3

ANTICIPATION GUIDE

Self	Statement	Group
	1. All explorers find new places.	
	2. My sister is an explorer because she traveled through Europe last summer.	
	3. Readers are explorers.	
	4. Explorers find answers to questions.	

HANDOUT 1.4

WHO AM I?: AN EXPLORATION

Directions: Go on an exploration (scavenger hunt) in your bedroom, house, or neighborhood. Write down answers that will give clues about what's important to you. As you work, ask yourself: *Who am I? What do I care about?* If there's a category you can't complete, use your imagination!

3 most important things	An object that reminds you of a special memory	1–2 soft things	1–2 hard things
1. 2. 3.	Object: Memory:	1. 2.	1. 2.
Something that came from out of town	**Something from nature**	**Something manmade**	**Something you made**
Something that will fit in your hand	**Something that will not fit in your hand**	**Something that used to belong to someone else**	**Your favorite gift**

HANDOUT 1.4, CONTINUED

QUESTIONS FOR CONSIDERATION

1. What do these items say about me?

2. What is it that I care about?

LESSON 2 Concept Exploration

MATERIALS

- ✓ Student journals
- ✓ Handout 1.4: Who Am I?: An Exploration
- ✓ Handout 2.1: Concept Cards (cut out prior to lesson)
- ✓ Handout 2.2: Letter to Parents

Research is an organized and systematic way of finding answers to questions.

OBJECTIVES

Students will:

- ✓ synthesize knowledge for communication,
- ✓ compare and contrast various concepts, and
- ✓ formulate hypotheses.

- Expedition
- Concept

SEQUENCE

WARM UP

1. Talk with students concerning the concept they examined yesterday, exploration. Hold a short question-and-answer session asking students questions such as: *Who is an explorer? What makes an explorer?*
2. Review the definition of *exploration* that the class created in the previous lesson. Explain that *exploration* is a *concept* and today they will be

investigating other concepts that will play important roles in this unit of study.

Concept (noun): A concept refers to an abstract, universal category of objects or ideas with similar attributes. Often, a concept is represented by a single word, such as conflict, exploration, metaphor or classification, or a few words, such as rite of passage or hero's journey. Concepts are important because they help us understand and organize key information within and across topics and disciplines.

DISCUSSION: HOMEWORK

Remind students to save this handout and brainstorming exercise. They will need it for future lessons.

3. Ask students to get out their results from their exploration (Handout 1.4). Have students read through their responses to see if they notice any themes or categories.
4. Ask: *What are some big issues you might be concerned about? Brainstorm topics that are related to the articles you found in your bedroom or home. Do you think others might be interested in this, too? Based on your findings, try to answer the question: "Who am I?"*

The idea of the exploration is to have students find topics that genuinely interest them. At the conclusion of this activity, students should have 3–5 topics of interest. For example, a student who found a dolphin stuffed animal, a shark's tooth, and a picture of a family vacation to the beach might want to think about topics such as oil spills, global warming, or marine life. A student who wrote about a soccer jersey and awards trophy may be interested in how countries are selected to compete in the World Cup. Students will need assistance to work toward these ideas—but they need only be ideas at this point.

ACTIVITY: CONCEPT MANIPULATION

Based on your observations during Lesson 1, pair students by readiness for this lesson's concept investigation and principle construction activity. For example, put the two students who showed the deepest understanding about exploration together and the students who showed the shallowest understanding about exploration together. This should help you determine students' depth of understanding and which group might need the most support.

5. In pairs, have students pick one of their home bases to work from. Distribute Handout 2.1: Concept Cards. (Cut these out prior to the lesson.) Make sure each pair/group has a full set of cards. You may decide to use two sets of concept cards, so that students with less complex levels of understanding have cards with the following terms: *writer, reader,*

explorer, purpose, questions, clues, steps, and *knowledge,* or other simpler terms.

6. Identify these as concept cards and quickly define *concept* again. Explain that this activity will help students think more about concepts and words that are commonly associated with them. Read each card aloud and have one of the students in each pair hold up their matching card. You may want to go over some definitions if necessary.
7. Instruct students to pair words that they think "match," are "complementary," or just "work well together." Before students get to work, model a Think Aloud process of pairing two cards together. This grouping should be very revealing about what kind of exposure the students have had to these words/concepts. You will probably need to provide a lot of support and suggestions during this grouping stage. Emphasize that there is no single correct answer to this exercise, but that different pairs of words could go together in different ways. You might encourage more advanced students to reuse cards so that they come up with more than three pairs.

Ensure each word makes it on a poster at least once. This may require you to encourage some students to pose different sentences than they initially chose. Most students will probably feel comfortable with the words *reader* and *writer*. Encourage those who wrote great sentences for the more difficult words like *perspective* and *contribution* to share their creations.

Think Aloud: Model a metacognitive dialogue with yourself about your thought process concerning pairing the concepts. You will use this strategy quite often throughout the unit.

8. Once all pairs have sorted their cards, instruct the students to create sentences for their paired cards; that is, they should try to come up with a sentence that contains both words in the pair, and which shows how the words go together. Model this sentence creation for them. Perhaps choose two more difficult words to pair. Explain to students why you paired the words you did. On the board, write a sentence (ideally a relationship sentence) using both words. Examples include:
   - ✓ People have different *perspectives* about what *contributions* are important to our society.
   - ✓ *Writers* have different *purposes* when they write for different audiences.
   - ✓ Being an *explorer* means going on a *journey.*

9. Give students time to create these sentences. Each student should write the sentences in his or her journal—even though partners will write identical sentences. Monitor students' progress informally and provide support as required.
10. Ask each pair to determine their best sentence and rewrite it on a piece of chart paper or poster paper. Each pair should share their sentence with the class and post it somewhere in the room. (You may want to make this one bulletin board area.)

11. After students share their sentences, ask them to predict what they might be going to study throughout the unit.

INSTRUCTION: KNOWLEDGE EXPEDITION

12. Tell students they are going to be participating in a knowledge expedition, and ask if anyone has any ideas about what that may mean. Write "knowledge expedition" on the board. Spend some time dissecting the word expedition.

Expedition (noun): a. A journey undertaken by a group of people with a definite objective: an expedition against the enemy stronghold; a scientific expedition to the South Pole; b. The group undertaking such a journey. (n.d.)

- You might run into a time issue at this point. You can save your personal topic think aloud until next class if that works better.
- Please don't view the timelines for each lesson as rigid and definite, you can always finish lessons the following class.

13. Explain that students will have the opportunity to determine what they would like to explore. Throughout the unit they will learn how to search for and uncover important information. Share that you are going to be exploring as well!

Through a Think Aloud, model how you will determine your research question. The following scripted section serves as a guide for you. You are encouraged to use your own interests and ideas.

- Say: *I have lots of things that I am interested in. I really love [going to the beach].* (Write [beach] on the board.) *You know, maybe just brainstorming a list of all the things I am interested in could be the first step in getting my ideas out.* (You will want to make sure the topic "Explorers of America" is on the board if that is what you have chosen.)
- Brainstorm on the board while you think aloud. Don't overwhelm students with a massive list, but model how one idea spurs another. Once you have about 10 topics on the board, stop generating ideas, stand back, and review your list.
- Say: *I know that scientists and historians investigate and explore questions. That is how they conduct their research. There is an unanswered question that they attempt to answer. Scientists often conduct laboratory experiments to test if certain medicines will help people get better. For example, a question a scientist might ask is: Does this new medicine help patients avoid getting a cold? And historians often ask questions about why something happened. For example, a historian might ask: What factors of the presidential campaign influenced Obama's victory? So I want to look at my list here and determine what questions I have about these topics.*
- Use the think-aloud strategy to eliminate topics that just won't work—those that you can't turn into researchable questions. You will want to end up with: *Who really discovered America?* Use this question if you choose to use the materials provided in this unit. If you choose your own topic, be sure to find appropriate resources throughout the unit.

14. Tell students it is their turn to brainstorm all the areas they are interested in. Remind students that researchable questions are (1) highly interesting to the researcher, (2) able to be researched given available

resources and time, and (3) not too big and not too small. Often the most interesting research questions have no clear answer. In their journals, encourage students to jot down people, places, and events that are interesting to them. Prompt them to think about things that they have learned that they'd like to know more about. Give students time to think, talk, and record. Provide some time for students to turn to their neighbors and share their lists so far. Encourage students to look back to their Who am I?: An Exploration (Handout 1.4) for ideas.

- The "Who really discovered America?" topic is only an example for you to use along with the questions, links, and resources provided throughout the unit. That way you will have more time to adequately differentiate rather than look for appropriate materials.
- You may want to limit the subject area students will work in during this research project. You might want to limit it to science topics or social studies topics, or just studying people. Decide what will be best for you and your students. Remember that the more students are interested in their topic, the more they will stay motivated and get the most out of this unit.

CLOSE

15. Ask students to consider and discuss the following questions:
    - ✓ Are readers explorers? Why?
    - ✓ Are writers explorers? Why?
    - ✓ When are teachers explorers?
    - ✓ When are students explorers?

HOMEWORK

16. Instruct students to go home and talk with someone about their knowledge expedition. They will spend the next few weeks investigating a topic of interest to them (as long as it is teacher approved) and will want to make sure they have considered many potential topics. Send home a brief letter to parents informing them of what will take place during this unit of study and how they might offer assistance. Distribute Handout 2.2: Letter to Parents or use it for ideas of what to include in this letter.

PREPARATION: FOR NEXT LESSON

17. Prepare three sample texts about the discovery of America or another chosen theme (short articles or book excerpts), suitable for three different readiness levels:
    - ✓ Sample Text 1 needs to be of average readability (perhaps instructional level for most), but even more importantly it needs to contain various organizational structures like: bold and/or italicized words, section headings, captions, pictures or graphs, etc.
    - ✓ Sample Text 2A needs to be at an independent reading level for most students. Whiteout the section headings. Rewrite (or type and tape) the list of section headings at the bottom of the article, but do not put them in order.
    - ✓ Sample Text 2B needs to be the exact same text as 2A; however, do **not** add the section headings to the bottom of 2B.

HANDOUT 2.1

CONCEPT CARDS

WRITER

READER

EXPLORER

PERSPECTIVE

CONTRIBUTION

JOURNEY

PURPOSE

SYSTEM

HANDOUT 2.2

LETTER TO PARENTS

Greetings!

We are about to begin a new and exciting journey. For the next 4 weeks, our fifth graders will no longer just be students; they are going to be practicing researchers working to become an expert in a topic of their choice! Because this is such an undertaking, we could really use your help. Below is a list of ways you can help your researcher be successful in his or her endeavor.

- If your researchers have Internet access at home, they will most likely want to use it for further research. A watchful eye and support for their online work will probably be necessary.
- Send in any old issues of National Geographic, Smithsonian, travel magazines, or other resources that might be helpful.
- Ask your researchers how their research is coming along. Talk about what they are finding and what barriers are impeding their progress.
- Take your researchers to the public library. Help them locate and access resources not available at the school library.
- Provide your researchers with opportunities to engage in all kinds of resources related to their topic: museums, movies, documentaries, personal interviews with real experts, etc.
- Provide a helping hand in the classroom. Each researcher will be working to find answers to his or her own questions. An extra adult or two would ensure students get the individual support they are going to need.
- Help out during the Research Gala. At the end of this unit of study, the students will present their findings at a Research Gala.

Please feel free to e-mail or call me if you have some time to volunteer or if you have particular questions about this unit. Thank you in advance for your time and support.

Sincerely,

LESSON 3 Fiction and Nonfiction: What's the Difference?

MATERIALS

- ✓ Student research portfolios
- ✓ Student journals
- ✓ Explorer's Cart: A large collection of books from the library
- ✓ Three sample texts (*Note:* See Preparation section at the end of Lesson 2)
- ✓ Handout 3.1: Big6 Research Handbook (hole-punched for use in 3-ring binder)
- ✓ Appendix A1: Big6 Instructions
- ✓ Appendix A2: Big6 Research Process Poster (for display in the classroom; optional)

- Purposes and perspectives influence how readers and writers ("explorers") interact with texts.
- Readers can use strategies and structure to make meaning from texts.
- Research is an organized and systematic way of finding answers to questions.

OBJECTIVES

Students will:

- ✓ sort and classify texts by genre, and
- ✓ determine text features.

- Fiction
- Nonfiction

For the Explorer's Cart:

- Ensure a variety of text levels matching students' independent reading levels. Try to assemble these texts before you begin teaching the unit. You may want to elicit the help of the school librarian.
- Collect resources on the exploration of America. Include texts on Columbus, Ericson, Vespucci, etc. Also include other texts about explorations/expeditions. Include primarily nonfiction texts, but some fiction or historical fiction pieces as well.
- Aim for a fairly substantial collection (at least 20 books—more is better). Keep these texts in your classroom.

SEQUENCE

INSTRUCTION: THE EXPLORER'S HANDBOOK

1. Distribute Handout 3.1 and explain to students that this book is a tool to help with their new job. Just like plumbers, mechanics, doctors, and scientists have tools, so do researchers—and that is the role they will be taking on in the next few weeks. Each day they will work like real researchers, searching, uncovering, interpreting, organizing, and presenting information.
2. Researchers work with a plan. Ask students what they think would happen if an architect worked without a plan. How about a lawyer? How about a researcher?
3. Have students put their name on their handbook. Explain why it is called a Big6 Handbook (it provides a six-step plan to conduct research). Explain each step (see Appendix A1) and have students fill in the Become an Explorer page. They can use this as a guide throughout the unit.
4. **Step 1: Task Definition:** Work through the task definition page with the students. You will want students to copy word for word what they are supposed to do. Also, have them jot down all of their areas of interest. Students should use their top 3–5 topics (derived from Handout 1.4, along with their brainstorming session in Lesson 2). If they feel they have a question in mind, tell them they can write it in the bottom box but it is not necessary to complete at this time.
5. Ask: *Why it is important for researchers (like doctors, lawyers, and historians) to be very clear on their task definition? In other words, why do researchers need to know exactly what they are supposed to do?*

On the Become an Explorer page, students will copy the bulleted questions from the Big6 Research Process poster (Appendix A2). For example, in the box beside Task Definition, students should write three questions: *What is the problem/task? What information do I need to solve the problem? How will I present my findings?*

Task Definition: By investigating various nonfiction resources using the Big6 research method, I will uncover the answer to my research question. I will then share my findings with an audience in the form of a paper, presentation, or performance.

6. Explain to students that once they have a general sense of their research topics, they will learn strategies for understanding how to develop a research question and eventually answer it. Engage students in a discussion that might demonstrate this process. Use index cards and have students collaborate on answers to the following questions: *What did Columbus need to learn before setting out on his voyage? What did Bill Gates need to know before creating Windows? What would a meteorologist need to know before flying into a hurricane? What would a farmer need to know before planning a new crop?*

7. When discussing students' responses, reinforce the importance of planning in all of the above examples. Farmers, for example, must plan for the type of soil, rainfall, and the market of any given crop.
8. **Step 2: Information Seeking Strategies:** Discuss what nonfiction is. For some students this may be a review but understanding this is essential to the unit. Point out examples that are all around them: books, lunch menus, maps, magazines, letters to parents, etc. Define *nonfiction*: It gives information. It explains, informs, or persuades. Give students a few minutes to analyze their current piles, discuss, and make changes.
9. Create a chart titled "Characteristics of Nonfiction Texts." Work with students to create a list of features that makes nonfiction different than fiction. Ask them to examine the books in front of them to help with this task. Elicit responses and record everything that makes sense. When kids give a text feature, ask them why that feature is important (e.g., how does it help the reader?). Characteristics may include:
   - ✓ Based on true information
   - ✓ Information is accurate
   - ✓ Most experts agree on the content
   - ✓ Helps answer questions based on fact

- You may want to create a large poster with the definition of *nonfiction* on it and list examples. (You could use chart paper for this.) Leave it up throughout the entire unit.
- If you want students to record this list in their journals, have them do it during the instruction. However, the writing might distract them from fully understanding the big picture. Also, this chart paper will be posted in the room so the students can refer to it as needed.

10. Explain to students that these features are clues. These clues will help them explore and navigate nonfiction texts.

Explain to students that you are going to focus on nonfiction in their knowledge expedition. Remind students about the knowledge expedition that you introduced yesterday.

11. **Step 3: Location and Access:** Ask: *Where do you think we are going to begin locating and accessing the resources we need?* (School library.) *Where else can we go to find resources?*
12. Explain to students that they are probably going to the library for this unit with a different purpose than in the past. Past trips were probably to get fiction books for entertainment or to conduct research on topics selected by their teachers. Ask students what this new purpose may be (i.e., to find the answers to research questions).

Reiterate to students that their purpose of accessing library materials is to find information.

13. Take students to the library and show them around. Point out the magazines, newspapers, fiction books, nonfiction books, encyclopedias. You will want to show them how to look up terms in an encyclopedia. Focus on:

- ✓ Index
- ✓ Table of contents
- ✓ Copyright date location
- ✓ Computer-based card catalog search
- ✓ Finding information in an encyclopedia

INSTRUCTION: EXPLORING TEXT FEATURES

When you instruct students to turn-n-talk, they are to turn to a neighbor (consider telling them who their turn-n-talk neighbor is so no one is left out) and discuss the question. This ensures that every student is accountable for verbalizing an answer, and you can scan the room for a quick assessment of puzzled or confident faces.

14. Distribute Sample Text 1. Explain to students that they will look at articles about the discovery of America, as well as practice strategies that will help them get a better understanding of what they are reading.
15. Instruct students to examine the organizational features of Sample Text 1. Tell students to take a moment to skim the page, but do not read the article. Ask: *What kinds of "helpers" do the authors of this article use to help us better understand the text?* Take answers and make sure students identify the section headings.
16. Ask: *Why would an author use section headings? What are the purposes of section headings?* Apply a Turn-n-Talk strategy: *How many purposes for section headings can you think of?*

Possible purposes for section headings include to:

- tell the reader what is coming,
- transition from one section to next,
- provide a preview for whole text,
- hint to the main idea,
- help the reader organize ideas, and
- allow reader to make connections before reading.

17. Have students share their ideas and compile a list on the board or chart paper.
18. Read Sample Text 1 aloud and invite the students to consider other reasons for using section headings. Ask: *Is our initial list sufficient?* Share new ideas after reading aloud.

Assign students to one of two tasks. Students who have shown to be savvy in the areas of research in this unit *or* in reading comprehension in previous units will engage in a more challenging task. Depending upon your class, this may be a fairly small group. The rest of the class will engage in the second task. Explain that all students will read the same texts and have the same goal; they will just reach the goal in different ways.

19. Distribute Sample Text 2A and 2B to the appropriate groups (2A for lower-readiness students, 2B for higher-readiness students).

20. Tell students that for the next activity they are going to be reading detectives. Instruct students to look at the text. Ask: *What seems to be missing?* (Section headings.) Explain that their goal for this activity is to figure out what the section headings should be.
21. Read the article aloud. Decide if you want to stop at the end of each section and have students figure out and discuss their section heading choice—or wait until the end and have students work through it and discuss for an extended portion of time.
22. Offer students the chance to share their heading choices and compare to other groups. Ask: *What new information have we learned about the discovery of America?*

Discussion Opportunity: Compare Group B's original section headings to the ones Group A chooses from the list at the bottom of their text.

CLOSE

23. Make sure that students understand that nonfiction texts are also influenced by perspective and purpose. Provide these examples (or others) as facts—someone's birthday, land masses, continents, presidents—versus opinion—grass is green, dogs are good pets, technology is helpful, exercise is healthy, ice cream is bad for you.
24. With these examples, invite students to "poke holes" in the above arguments (grass isn't green during a drought, some people are allergic to dogs, doctors warn about exercise for some, ice cream can be good for those needing more dairy, etc.).

You will reflect on this brief activity in Lesson 6 as students are learning about thin versus thick questions.

PREPARATION: FORMATIVE ASSESSMENT 2

25. In their journals or as an exit card, have students answer three of the first five questions listed below. Have all students answer the sixth question.
    - ✓ What is one difference between fiction and nonfiction?
    - ✓ What is the purpose of nonfiction?
    - ✓ What is the Big6? (How is this method a system?)
    - ✓ How will section headings in information texts help you find the answer to your research question?
    - ✓ Why do authors of informational texts use section headings? What's this feature's purpose?
    - ✓ What does the following statement mean?: Research is an organized and systematic way to find answers to questions.

26. **Using the assessment data:** Read journal responses before the next lesson to get an idea of who may be struggling and who may need more of a challenge. Read and provide feedback on students' Research Handbooks. Make notes about students' developing understandings at this point in the unit.

HANDOUT 3.1

BIG6 RESEARCH HANDBOOK

BECOME AN **EXPLORER**

BIG6 RESEARCH HANDBOOK

YOUR NAME

HANDOUT 3.1, CONTINUED

BECOME AN **EXPLORER**

TASK DEFINITION	→	
INFORMATION SEEKING STRATEGIES	→	
LOCATION AND ACCESS	→	
USE OF INFORMATION	→	
SYNTHESIS	→	
EVALUATION	→	

HANDOUT 3.1, CONTINUED

STEP 1: TASK DEFINITION

1. What is the problem/task?

2. What information do I need to solve the problem?

3. How will I present my findings? (Format)

HANDOUT 3.1, CONTINUED

STEP 2: INFORMATION SEEKING STRATEGIES

In the space below, make a list of all the possible sources in which you could find the answer to your question or information on your topic.

STEP 3: LOCATION AND ACCESS

In the space below, make a list of all the places you can find these sources. Your school library is No. 1, but where else can you go?

HANDOUT 3.1, CONTINUED

STEP 4: USE OF INFORMATION

You will receive the "Researcher's Notebook" for use during this step. You also will receive the "Research Gala Rubric" for use during this step.

STEP 5: SYNTHESIS

In the space below, write or sketch how you will show your results. Will you write a paper, give a presentation, or put on a performance?

STEP 6: EVALUATION

You will receive the Research Gala Rubric for use during this step.

Note. Adapted from *Big6*™ by Michael B. Eisenberg and Robert E. Berkowitz, 1987, retrieved from http://www.big6.com. Copyright 1987 Michael B. Eisenberg and Robert E. Berkowitz. Adapted with permission.

LESSON

4 What Do I Know and Where Do I Go?

MATERIALS

- ✓ Access to library
- ✓ Handout 3.1: Big6 Research Handbook
- ✓ Handout 4.1: KWL Chart: The Discovery of America
- ✓ Handout 4.2: KWL Chart

- Research is an organized and systematic way of finding answers to questions.
- Values, experiences, and motivation contribute to the development of an explorer's (reader's) perspective and purpose.

OBJECTIVES

Students will:

- ✓ access prior knowledge through discussion, and
- ✓ compile a comprehensive list of research sources.

SEQUENCE

INSTRUCTION: KWL

1. Review your research question (Who really discovered America?) with the students, and explain that researchers don't blindly wander through the library to find books on a topic of interest; they take time to figure out what they already know in relation to the current investigation. Ask students to help you determine what you (and they) already know about the discovery of America.

- Have your KWL chart filled out ahead of time so when students are filling in theirs you are able to walk around the room to observe and support.
- Put these KWLs in a safe place. You will need them later in the unit.
- Keep the chart paper KWL on display in the classroom. As you learn important information concerning your investigation, add to the L column. Share these findings with the class. Your excitement and motivation for your investigation will have quite an impact on your students.

Group students into similar readiness pairs for the following activity. Pair those students who have shown a strong interest in social studies/history together, based on your observations from previous lessons. You want to put these "social studies thinkers" together to engage each other in dialogues that trigger recall of past learning experiences concerning the discovery of America. For the pairs of students who have shown little prior knowledge and/or interest in the topic, you will provide support during the activity with probing questions.

2. Distribute Handout 4.1: KWL Chart: The Discovery of America. Explain the purpose of a KWL chart is to figure out exactly what you already *know* about a subject and also decide what you *want* to know or *wonder* about. Explain to students that at the end of your exploration into the discovery of America, you will fill out the last column of this chart by writing what you *learned* during the investigation.
3. Ask students for their help in determining what they collectively know about the discovery of America. Instruct each pair to fill in the K column. Give students the time you feel is necessary to do this task.
4. Have students share their knowledge. You can create a chart paper KWL using three sheets of chart paper—one for the K, one for the W, and one for the L. Make sure that you add your knowledge to K column as well.
5. Instruct students on the purpose of the W column. Ask: *If you were studying/researching the discovery of America what would you like to know? For example, after so many years, why can't historians agree on who discovered America?*
6. Give students the time you feel is necessary to do this task. Have pairs share their questions as you write them on the classroom KWL chart. Explain when the L column will be filled in and ask the students: *Now that we know what we know and what we want to know, where do we go from here?* Collect student copies of Handout 4.1.

As students work through the research process and begin to identify topics of interest, you may need to provide guidance and feedback to some students who need help identifying appropriate topics of interest.

ACTIVITY: KWL . . . THEIR TURN!

7. Have students turn to Step 1: Task Definition on Handout 3.1. Explain that you have provided each student with some suggestions or feedback concerning their topics of interest.
8. Explain to students that they helped you create a KWL chart on your topic. Now, they will be creating a KWL for their own research topic(s). Students should narrow their research topics to two options at this point.

- Students should look back at Handout 1.4, along with other brainstorming sessions to determine the final topics for investigation. Your feedback should also help students move in the right direction.
- The point of the KWL chart is for students to determine if they have enough questions (W) to launch an inquiry. If not, they may need to switch topics. Your involvement will be critical at this step.
- Students will soon have the task of developing a research question from a research topic.

9. Distribute Handout 4.2: KWL Chart and tell students they are responsible for filling out the K and W columns of this chart. As students who already have strong research topics begin work on the KWL, meet with the students who had a "see me" notation on their Research Handbook (Handout 3.1).
10. Give students sufficient time to complete the first two columns of their KWL chart. Spend about 5 minutes sharing one thing each child wrote on his or her KWL chart. You can do this as a whole class, in pairs, or in small groups. Have students place their completed KWL in their research binder.

INSTRUCTION: BACK TO STEP 2: INFORMATION SEEKING STRATEGIES

11. Have students return to Step 2 in the Big6 process: Information Seeking Strategies. Explain that multiple sources must be accessed during a research investigation. Ask: *What do I mean by multiple sources? Why would a researcher look in many different places for the answer to one question?* You can use the turn-n-talk strategy here. Share ideas after the brief paired discussion.
12. Tell students that today they are going to make a master list of all of the sources they can access to respond to their topics. Remember: Students do not yet have a research question. (This is by design!) The KWL and silent search will help students determine if their "topic" lends itself to an inquiry. Dissect the word *source* and its multiple meanings.
13. Prepare a sheet of chart paper, titled "Research Sources."
14. In order to compile an accurate and extensive list you will take the students on a Silent Search. Ask students: *Where in our school would you probably find the most sources to answer your research question?* (The library.) Tell students that they will be going on a Silent Search of their library, and they have a very important goal during this mini-investigation. They will only spend 3 silent minutes in the library. When they are there, they will jot down all of the possible sources and places researchers can look to find answers to their questions. You can say, for example:

You may want to invite the school librarian to teach this part of the lesson, and you may want to add another day for the continuation of this lesson. Students are going to need significant support in finding the materials they need if they don't have a lot of previous experience using the school library. Your librarian is likely the best resource for teaching students how to access various sources of information.

I will give you the first item you can put on your list right now . . . books! That was an easy one, I know; however, there are many other sources available to you.

15. Require students to take their Big6 Research Handbooks (Handout 3.1) and jot down their list on the back of it. Ask if there are questions about this Silent Search. Stress to the students the importance of being quiet in the library and not disturbing any other workers/researchers.
16. After the Silent Search, compile a resource list. Have students write this list in their Big6 Research Handbooks under Information Seeking Strategies. Use chart paper and keep the list up throughout the unit. At this point, students might forget strategies such as speaking to experts, visiting museum exhibits, or other strategies beyond books and online sources. You will probably add to it as the students uncover other possible sources.

Based on student responses to the Computer/Library Preassessment (Handout 1.2), along with the quick trip to the library in Lesson 3, you may decide to eliminate the Silent Search if your students seem to be comfortable with the resources found there.

PREPARATION: FORMATIVE ASSESSMENT 3

17. In their journals or as an exit card, have students answer one of the first two questions listed below. Have all students answer the third question.
    - ✓ Before you begin looking for the answers to your research question, what should you do first?
    - ✓ What is a source?
    - ✓ How does what you already know about a topic (your prior knowledge) influence how you will go about researching it?

Resources found on the Silent Search may include: books, magazines, newspapers, maps, encyclopedias, computers, the librarian, etc.

18. **Using the assessment data:** In the next lesson, students will use the Internet. Refer to student responses on the Computer/Library Preassessment (Handout 1.2) to determine their technological needs and know-how. This will help you plan to differentiate for students based on their computer and Internet readiness. You will also need to reserve a computer lab, library, or laptop cart for the next lesson.

- Journal entries will serve as informal assessment tools for you to determine flexible groups throughout the unit. In addition, you should provide feedback on entries. Give students written feedback on their responses. Pose questions to further their thinking.
- The third question was not directly taught; however, it will yield important information concerning each student's understanding of the current concepts and principles.

HANDOUT 4.1

KWL CHART: THE DISCOVERY OF AMERICA

THE DISCOVERY OF AMERICA		
WHAT DO I **K**NOW?	WHAT DO I **W**ANT TO KNOW?	WHAT DID I **L**EARN?

HANDOUT 4.2

KWL CHART

TOPIC:

WHAT DO I **K**NOW?	WHAT DO I **W**ANT TO KNOW?	WHAT DID I **L**EARN?

LESSON 5 Texts on the Internet: Friend or Foe?

MATERIALS

- ✓ Large index cards (one per student)
- ✓ Student journals
- ✓ Access to a computer lab, library, or laptop cart
- ✓ Textbook (one per student). Your social studies or science textbook would be ideal. If you do not have one, try borrowing from another class/grade (fourth/fifth grade or higher). The students will not be reading the text; they will be examining its organizational features.
- ✓ A print source (a textbook would be best) with a chapter or a few pages about Columbus or the discovery of America
- ✓ Two webpages about the discovery of America, a certain explorer, or even just about history in general. Choose two sites that are high quality (with menus and links that work), such as:
  - Whole-group investigation site: http://www.history.com
  - Small-group investigation site: http://www.si.edu/kids/
- ✓ Other useful websites such as:
  - http://www.socialstudiesforkids.com/subjects/explorers.htm
  - http://www.cln.org/themes/explorers.html
- ✓ Handout 3.1: Big6 Research Handbook
- ✓ Handout 5.1: Organizational Features Chart

- Readers can use strategies and structures to make meaning from texts.
- Research is an organized and systematic way of finding answers to questions.

OBJECTIVES

Students will:

- ✓ identify and compare text features within textbooks and webpage formats,
- ✓ use an organizational system to locate information,
- ✓ determine the accuracy and reliability of online sources, and
- ✓ identify appropriate resources to answer research question

- Print and nonprint texts

SEQUENCE

WARM UP

1. Distribute one index card per student. Tell students to put their name on it. Reassure them that this is not a quiz or graded assignment. It is actually a task to help you, the teacher, design better lessons and activities. Remind students that yesterday you talked about a very important feature in nonfiction texts (section headings). Instruct students to write on the index card: (1) the name of this text feature and (2) one purpose of the feature.
2. Walk around the room as they write to get a quick idea of their understanding from yesterday.
3. Collect the cards. Have students share their answers to the questions. Clear up any misunderstandings concerning section headings.

You can provide minimal "hints" to jog students' memories.

INSTRUCTION: PRINT VS. NONPRINT TEXT

4. Tell students that yesterday they examined print text, but today they are also going to look at nonprint text.

Ask: *What is considered nonprint text?* You want to get students talking about online resources/texts. Ask them what kinds of things they go online to "look up"?

5. Explain to students that you have been online investigating many nonprint resources for your knowledge expedition: Who really discovered America? Tell students that you have found many similarities between print materials and nonprint materials.

6. Pull your chosen website up on the screen. In addition, have a textbook ready with a bookmark in the Columbus section and the Table of Contents.

- Share with students that you think this website *might* be helpful in answering your research question. Explain that you know there is a lot more to this site than just this opening webpage. Ask: *Does anyone have any idea how I uncover more information in this site?* (Possible answers: Scroll down, click on the links in the text, click on the links in the menu. You want the students to identify the menu.)
- Spend a few minutes showing the students how a web page menu functions like a book's table of contents. Discuss the similarities and differences in these two features. However, do get to the bottom line: They both serve the same purpose.

ACTIVITY: INVESTIGATION IN PAIRS

Use the assessment data from Formative Assessment 3 to determine student pairs for this activity.

7. Distribute Handout 5.1: Organizational Features Chart to pairs of students.

Some students may require extensive support to complete this task.

2E

8. Pairs are going to work as expert explorers. One will be the Textbook Explorer, the other will be the Webpage Explorer. (Tell students who is who.) Both have equal and important jobs. The goal is to complete Handout 5.1 by comparing a textbook to a webpage. Walk the students through the first row, using the table of contents as the feature to compare. Ask: *What text feature did I just compare in the textbook and the webpage?* The table of contents and menu.
9. Show the students how to fill out the chart and ask if there are any questions. Students need computers with Internet access to complete this chart. Take them to a library or computer lab or assign them to computers in the classroom.
10. Instruct students to open an Internet browser and provide a website you want them to explore. It should be a site concerning the discovery of America or another site that connects to something the students are currently studying. You want to make sure the webpage is organized well

- If computer access is a challenge, project a webpage for the class to view as a group.
- Write the web address you want students to view on the top of the Organizational Features Chart *before* you make copies. This way, students will not make an error when transcribing it from the board.

and that the students can see the similarities and differences between the website and their print source (the textbook).

ACTIVITY: INDEPENDENT WEBSITE INVESTIGATION

11. Now students will look at two different websites. On their own, they will evaluate the website, and as a class, they will create a list describing the characteristics of a good website.
12. Direct students to the first website. Tell them to look closely at how the website is organized and note strengths/weaknesses. You may suggest that ease of access, adequate information, and user friendliness are some features they could start with.
13. After about 2–5 minutes, have students move on to the next website. When the time is up, ask: *Think about the website you examined. What makes it a good website?* As students share, make a list on the board/chart paper.

Possible responses for why to use these sites include that they are easy to read, are easy to navigate, are kid-friendly, have lots of pictures, have lots of information, have a main menu, have links that work, and are created by a reputable person/group.

14. Require students to look critically at the list. Explain that you want to create a class checklist to help researchers find quality online (nonprint) sources. Ask: *Why do we have to be very careful and critical about the information we find online?* Solicit answers. You may want to pose a comparison question about why we don't have to be as critical of textbooks as we do of online web pages.

Possible checklist questions include:

- Who created the website? What do we know about the author/ organization?
- Is there a main menu?
- Do all of the links work?
- Does the information seem accurate?
- Are their sources cited? Does the author say where he or she found the information he or she posted?

15. Have students add and delete criteria from the list on the board. Work with them until you think you have a workable list—one that is not too overwhelming but prompts them to look critically at web pages. You will want to change the criteria into answerable questions.
16. Demonstrate working through the checklist with the website you selected for your exploration concerning the discovery of America.

- You will pick out two websites for your students to evaluate. In order to compare and contrast, you can choose websites of varying levels of quality. Some suggestions:
    - http://www.kidsknowit.com
    - http://kids.nationalgeographic.com
    - http://www.cogito.org
    - http://www.homeworkhotline.org
- Getting to work on the computer is really fun for most students! You may need to keep students on task. Remind students that this is not the time to play games or read every article, but to evaluate the website as a potential resource.

17. Instruct students to find another site that they feel might be beneficial to their research, but this time they will evaluate the site using the checklist on the board/chart paper. Keep this posted in the room, or type it up to distribute to students for use during their research.
18. Tell students that they may want to record the URL(s) in their Big6 Research Handbooks so they can find it (them) again.

CLOSE

19. Give students a chance to peruse various websites (if the school has a filter) or http://www.kidsclick.org to see if they contain information helpful in answering their research questions. As they work, move from student to student quietly asking: *Why is critically evaluating a website with a checklist like the one we created a good idea?* Collect Handout 5.1.

- If you/the class has a webpage, you may link the website(s) beforehand. Then direct students to simply click on the link.
- Carefully review charts to see students' understanding of print and nonprint text features.

Some questions for class discussion include:

- What did you find during your comparison exploration? Which do you think is easier to use: a print or nonprint resource? Why? What might be some problems with using only print resources? Nonprint?
- Think about one website you explored today. What is good about this website? What is not so good about it?
- Why is it important to evaluate the websites we use?

Name: ____________________ Date: ____________

HANDOUT 5.1

ORGANIZATIONAL FEATURES CHART

TEXT FEATURE	WEBSITE FORMAT	PURPOSE OF FEATURE/FORMAT

LESSON 6

How to Create a Research Question

MATERIALS

- ✓ Large chart with eight columns with headings: Who, What, Where, When, Why, How, Which, and Other
- ✓ Sticky notes for student use
- ✓ Handout 6.1: Choosing Good Research Questions
- ✓ Handout 6.2: Good Research Question Checklist
- ✓ Handout 6.3: Research Question Chart
- ✓ Appendix A3: Choosing Good Research Questions Answer Key
- ✓ Appendix A4: Sample Think-Aloud
- ✓ Appendix A5: Research Flowchart

- Research is an organized and systematic way of finding answers to questions.
- Purposes and perspectives influence how readers and writers interact with text.

OBJECTIVES

Students will:

- ✓ use an organizational system to focus on the specifics of a topic,
- ✓ determine the difference between thick and thin questions, and
- ✓ identify appropriate purposes in reading texts for information.

SEQUENCE

INTRODUCTION

1. Say: *So far we've thought about our topics—what we know about that topic and what we hope to learn. We've also explored various types of texts and how they can be used as sources in our research. As a result,*

we know where we can find information and how to determine if that information is reliable. We've learned the essential steps for starting our exploration, so now it's time to narrow down our research topics and come up with good research questions. First, we'll try it together as a class. Then you'll have time to work on your own questions.

- Some students have received a certain amount of instruction on types of questions, usually in regard to asking questions about their reading. Students may be used to thinking of these two types of questions as "right there" questions—meaning that the answers can be found verbatim in the text—or inference questions that engage the reader's thinking.
- If students have not learned about these two general types of questions, a mini-lesson is suggested (see Figure 3). You may want to remind students about the closure activity you did in Lesson 3 (Fact vs. Opinion). "Are dogs colorblind?" would make for a thin question. However, "Do dogs make good pets?" would require the student to research the facts but also consider multiple viewpoints.

High-Consensus Questions (Thin Questions)	Low-Consensus Questions (Thick Questions)
Fact	Facts
One answer	Many answers
One viewpoint	Multiple viewpoints
Only one source necessary	Many sources necessary
Consensus on answer	Many opinions about answer
Answer found quickly	Answer found over time

FIGURE 3. THICK VERSUS THIN QUESTIONS.

2. Select a topic of interest to the students, one on which they will have quite a bit of background knowledge. (The sample chart [Appendix A5] uses the topic "whales.") Have the students brainstorm words associated with the topic. Remind students of the rules of brainstorming—come up with as many ideas as you can, piggyback on the ideas of others, be freewheeling, and defer judgment. Record their ideas on the board/chart paper. Follow up with some convergent thinking about which words are important to the topic. You may want to underline or highlight the words deemed important. Then ask students to think of questions about the topic, using the important words that remain from the brainstorming session and other words as they wish.

- If students need additional reinforcement, you can demonstrate this process using your question: Who really discovered America?
- Note that not all good research questions are "why" and "how" questions and that not all "where" or "when" questions make poor research questions. Depending upon the level of insight demonstrated by your students, you may introduce questions that challenge such dichotomous thinking, such as "Who really discovered America?," "Who really invented the automobile?," or "Where can the oldest remains of prehistoric humans be found?" These are examples of questions that, despite beginning with "who" and "where," are open-ended because of the amount of controversy they generate and the number of possible answers to be found, depending on different points of view.
- Be certain that students do not confuse questions that are difficult to answer with those that would be suitable for research. For example, the question, "How many people live on Earth?" is difficult to answer, because it changes every second and there is no way to count physically all the people on Earth at one time. It would not be a good research question, however, because there is one correct answer. Another way to guide student thinking about difficult versus researchable questions is to ask them to imagine that they actually could figure out the answer (i.e., that there was a way to count all the people on Earth in one second). What would be the point of research, then? The answer would be just a number. There would be no need to synthesize information, no further questions to explore, no difference of opinions or viewpoints. Such a question does not require use of the research process.

3. Distribute sticky notes. Ask students to record their questions on the sticky notes, one question per note. Check with students as they write to minimize repetition.
4. Post the large chart you made. Have students place each of their questions in the correct column of the chart according to its "question word" (usually the first word).
5. Add your own questions to empty columns; fill in with questions that match/don't match the "good research question" criteria on the checklist, so that there are examples and nonexamples with which to work. Thinking of questions in advance that fulfill and don't fulfill the criteria will help facilitate a rich discussion.
6. Say: *Remember that we have learned that research is an organized and systematic way of finding answers to questions. Based on what we have learned so far about research, what kinds of questions do you think would be the best kind to research?*
7. Use the questions on the chart to help students discover features that would/would not make good researchable questions. You might highlight the questions in different colors, or use different color dots to mark them—one color for those questions that the students think might be good to research, another for those they think are inappropriate for research, and another color for those questions they are unsure of or

about which there is disagreement. Establish these baseline qualities of a research question first:

- ✓ The question is one the student is interested in answering.
- ✓ The question is one to which the student does not already know the answer.
- ✓ The answer to the question is one that cannot be stated in one or a few words.

8. Let students discuss the questions in groups and then ask for volunteers from each group to pull off any questions that do not meet the criteria. Ask: *What do you notice about the categories of questions that are left?* (They are mostly "why" and "how" questions.) *Why would these be the best questions to research?* Guide students to the realization that a complex, open-ended question will help give a focus to their reading. Ask: *Do we need to add more criteria to this checklist?* See if students have other ideas for criteria or other ways to word the criteria.
9. Distribute Handout 6.1: Choosing Good Research Questions. Say: *It's important to have a good research question to guide your reading. Now, I'm going to give you a chance to practice your skills at determining good research questions. I have assigned you to different groups. You will examine 10 possible research questions.* (Heterogeneous grouping would work well here.) *Using the checklist, look at each question and decide as a group whether it meets the criteria for a good question or not. Mark "Yes" or "No" beside the question and give the reasons for your answer.*
10. Be sure to check the answers before proceeding to the next activity. An answer key is included (Appendix A3). If students need additional support, use the sample think-aloud (Appendix A4) to model how you might determine the merit of various questions about a topic.

CLOSE

11. Distribute Handout 6.3 (Research Question Chart). Students will use the chart as they attempt to write a research question with their own topics. By now, students should have one or two remaining topics. Tell students that the categories—who, what, etc.—are there to help them brainstorm questions.

PREPARATION: FOR NEXT LESSON

12. Review students' attempts at research questions and make comments. Asking for students to volunteer their questions (so that the group can discuss them) would be an optional closing activity or warm-up for the next lesson. This is a key lesson. With your support, they should

determine their research questions at this point in the unit. You may need to conduct one-on-one conferences with students. Once you have approved their questions, have students write their final research question on Step 1: Task Definition in their Big6 Research Handbook (Handout 3.1). This will be the research question they move forward with for the remainder of the unit.

HANDOUT 6.1

CHOOSING GOOD RESEARCH QUESTIONS

Directions: Read each of the following questions and mark if they are good researchable questions by putting a check mark in the box beside it. If the question is not a good research question, mark an X in the box and on the lines below the question, see if you can make it a better research question.

❑ 1. Who invented the pencil?

❑ 2. Why do many people want to eat organic food?

❑ 3. How does the iPod work?

❑ 4. What are all of the holidays celebrated around the world?

❑ 5. Who came up with the idea for cell phones?

❑ 6. Which sport is the best?

❑ 7. When is the best time to get a new pet?

❑ 8. Why do students have to take state tests in school?

❑ 9. How can we help endangered species?

❑ 10. Who won the Superbowl last year?

HANDOUT 6.2

GOOD RESEARCH QUESTION CHECKLIST

A good research question . . .

- ✓ is based on the interests of the researcher.
- ✓ has answers based on data.
- ✓ has adequate information available to help the researcher find answers (i.e., is not too specific).
- ✓ can be researched in the time available (i.e., is not too broad).
- ✓ requires discovery (does not have an obvious answer).
- ✓ takes time to answer.
- ✓ is a low-consensus/"thick" question (i.e., everyone may not agree on the answer).
- ✓ can be investigated from different viewpoints.
- ✓ requires the use of many resources.
- ✓ may have multiple correct answers.
- ✓ may be unanswerable (may not have an answer).
- ✓ may lead to further questions.
- ✓ requires the researcher to synthesize information.
- ✓ requires the researcher to explain the results.

These criteria can be thought of in three categories:

- criteria about the topic, or content, of the question;
- criteria about the method by which the question best can be answered, or the fit between the question and the research process; and
- criteria about the possible answer or result of answering the question.

HANDOUT 6.3

RESEARCH QUESTION CHART

Directions: Fill in the chart with the questions you have on your topic. Be sure to put your questions in the appropriate column according to the type of question it is.

Who	
What	
When	
Where	
Why	
How	
Which	
Other	

LESSON 7 Exploring Texts: Metacognition and Marking

MATERIALS

- ✓ Sticky notes (5–10 per student)
- ✓ Explorer's Cart
- ✓ Access to a computer lab, library, or laptop cart
- ✓ Handout 7.1: Columbus Reading: The Beginning
- ✓ Handout 7.2: INSERT Poster (also display a copy in classroom)

- Readers can use strategies and structure to make meaning from texts.
- Research is an organized and systematic way of finding answers to questions.

OBJECTIVES

Students will:

- ✓ monitor comprehension (metacognition),
- ✓ work cooperatively and independently to apply the INSERT strategy, and
- ✓ locate and access various library materials.

- Notation

SEQUENCE

INSTRUCTION: INSERT STRATEGY

1. Ask students: *Have you ever read something and realized after a couple of sentences that you have no idea what you've just read?*

- Read about the INSERT strategy at: https://www.ocps.net/cs/services/cs/currareas/read/IR/bestpractices/GL/INSERT.pdf
- The INSERT strategy template can be found at: http://www.readwritethink.org/files/resources/lesson_images/lesson230/insert.pdf
- You will want to plan your markings and think alouds ahead of time; however, you'll want them to look spontaneous.

If you think five different notations are too much for the students you are working with, take away one or two. Always keep "?" and "*".

Explain to students that they are going to learn a reading strategy called INSERT (**I**nteractive **N**otation **S**ystem for **E**ffective **R**eading and **T**hinking) that helps them monitor their own comprehension. This strategy will help them when they have to tackle difficult texts during their research. In this strategy you are actually supposed to write on the text! Talk with them about how students in college actually get to write in their books, so they use this kind of strategy all the time. Explain that they are going to practice the strategy first, and write directly on a copy of a text—but then they are going to implement this strategy with books they are not allowed to write in.

2. Distribute Handout 7.1: Columbus Reading and Handout 7.2: INSERT Poster. You may use another reading linked to your topic if you prefer.

Model the strategy:

- Read the text aloud and use the INSERT technique on Handout 7.1. Make sure you think aloud with every mark that you make. Make notations in the margins using the symbols on Handout 7.2.
- Stop halfway through the text or even sooner. Ask the students to describe what you just did. You want them to recognize the check mark, the exclamation point, the question mark, and the plus sign. You want to lead them to understanding what each of those signs signifies.
- Display the INSERT poster (Handout 7.2).
- Model the INSERT strategy through another small chunk of text. Again, debrief with the students.
- Have students practice the strategy. If you think the readability of the text is too difficult, read the text aloud to the kids, provide time for them to think about what you've read, and make an INSERT notation.
- Get students to talk about the purpose of the INSERT strategy. Why should they use it? When should they use it?

- You may want to modify this lesson and have students work in groups at this point. The extra support from a classmate might make trying the INSERT strategy a bit easier
- You may want to have copies of different one-page passages so students who can't find appropriate reading material have a back-up text.

ACTIVITY: INSERT WITH STICKY NOTES

3. Talk with students about the purpose of the INSERT strategy. Ask them when they think the use of this strategy would be most relevant to them. Talk about how great it would be to write on the text but that we are not allowed to do that with schoolbooks or library books. However, you

have a solution. Share with the students that sometimes when people read both fiction and nonfiction, they like to take notes. Not pages and pages of notes, but ideas here and there.

4. Model the sticky note strategy using one of the library books from the Explorer's Cart. Read aloud a section to your students and think aloud your INSERT notations. This time, write down your ideas on a sticky note and place it in the book. Show students that you leave the sticky note hanging out of the book a bit so you can easily find the page again.
5. Students will now independently practice the INSERT strategy. Encourage them to use a book from the Explorer's Cart or a book they are using for their knowledge expedition. Give students time to locate their text of choice as you pass out sticky notes (5–10 per student).
6. Monitor independent practice.

ACTIVITY: MAIDEN VOYAGE

7. For the second part of the lesson, you will take students to the library to do some initial exploration specific to their questions. Give the students a few guidelines before you head to the library. Possible guidelines could include but are not limited to:
   - ✓ Computers will not be a source you will access today.
   - ✓ Scout out various sources before settling down and reading one particular source.
   - ✓ If possible, sign out one or two books that you can keep in the classroom or take home to read. There is a reference cart for our class. Here you put books that aren't allowed to leave the library. (You may want to explain the purpose of the reference cart in greater detail.)

8. Explain to students that research is often hard and time-consuming. They will hit dead ends and may get frustrated. Professional researchers have the same problems and frustrations. Before you head to the library, examine the word *research* with the class. Ask students to dissect the word. Perhaps ask: *Do you see any smaller words in the big word research?* Help the kids work through and examine the word *research* and its definition.

- Research (noun): a detailed study of a subject, especially in order to discover (new) information or reach a (new) understanding.
- The term *research* is used to describe a number of similar and often overlapping activities involving a search for information. Ask: *How is the Big6 process an overlapping activity?*

- Make sure you schedule the library visit ahead of time. Also make sure the librarian is available to assist students.
- Ask the librarian if you can start a Reference Cart; this would stay in the library (not the Explorer's Cart in your room). Students who find valuable reference texts and want to work with a reference book for an extended period of time could put it on this cart. You may want to start out with a rule that each student can only have two reference books on the cart at one time.

9. Escort students to the library. Instruct students that once they've scouted the library and know what is available to them, they should sit down with one or two sources and silently read. There is no need to take notes yet. They just want to gain some general knowledge of their personal research topic.

- Try to be as hands-off as possible for the first 10 minutes. Let the students "fend for themselves." Watch carefully as the students try to navigate the library on their own. Notice who seems to have the most trouble with this new independence. After about 10 minutes, you and the librarian can "rescue" those who seem to be floundering.

- Gather students together at the end of the library visit (perhaps when you are back in the classroom), and give them a chance to share some of their experiences or findings with the group.

CLOSE

10. Close this lesson by returning to the students' journals. Remind students that self-reflection and self-monitoring are important to being an effective researcher. Invite students to respond to the following prompts:
    - ✓ What did you learn about your topic today?
    - ✓ What problems did you encounter today? How did you or might you solve these problems?

11. Make sure to read these journal entries before the next lesson.

Note. Elements of this lesson are adapted from *Guided Comprehension: Monitoring Using the INSERT Technique* by Sarah Dennis-Shaw, n.d., retrieved from: http://www.readwritethink.org/classroom-resources/lesson-plans/guided-comprehension-monitoring-using-230.html. Copyright ILA/NCTE, 2015. Adapted with permission.

HANDOUT 7.1

COLUMBUS READING: THE BEGINNING

Sailors are very fond of telling big stories about their own adventures or about far-off lands and countries. Columbus listened to many of these sea-stories, and heard many wonderful things about a very rich land away to the East that folks called Cathay.

If you look in your geography books, you will not find any such place on the map as Cathay, but you will find China, and that was what men in the time of Columbus called Cathay. They told very big stories about this far-off Eastern land. They said its kings lived in golden houses, that they were covered with pearls and diamonds, and that everybody there was so rich that money was as plentiful as the stones in the street.

This, of course, made the sailors and storekeepers very anxious to go to Cathay and get some of the gold, jewels, spices, and splendor for themselves. But Cathay was miles and miles away from Italy and Spain and France and England. It was away across the deserts and mountains and seas and rivers, and they had to give it up because they could not sail there.

At last a man whose name was Marco Polo really did go there, in spite of all the trouble it took. And when he got back his stories were so very surprising that men were all the more anxious to find a way to sail in their ships to Cathay and see it for themselves.

But of course they could not sail over the deserts and mountains, and they were very much troubled because they had to give up the idea, until the son of the king of Portugal, named Prince Henry, said he believed that ships could sail around Africa and so get to India or "the Indies" as they called that land, and finally to Cathay.

Just look at your map again and see what a long, long voyage it would be to sail from Spain and around Africa to India, China, and Japan. It is such a long sail that, as you know, the Suez Canal was dug some 20 years ago so that ships could sail through the Mediterranean Sea and out into the Indian Ocean, and not have to go away around Africa.

But when Columbus was a boy it was even worse than now, for no one really knew how long Africa was, or whether ships really could sail around it. But Prince Henry said he knew they could, and he sent out ships to try. He died before his Portuguese sailors, Bartholomew Diaz, in 1493, and Vasco de Gama, in 1497, at last did sail around it and got as far as "the Indies."

So while Prince Henry was trying to see whether ships could sail around Africa and reach Cathay in that way, the boy Columbus was listening to the stories the sailors told and was wondering whether some other and easier way to Cathay might not be found.

HANDOUT 7.2

INSERT POSTER

✓	I KNEW THAT
+	IMPORTANT NEW IDEA
!	WOW!
?	I DON'T UNDERSTAND
*	GO BACK TO THIS SPOT
☐ Create your own	

Note. Adapted from *INSERT Poster* by ReadWriteThink, n.d., retrieved from http://www.readwritethink.org/files/resources/lesson_images/lesson230/insert.pdf. Copyright 2003 IRA/NCTE. Adapted with permission.

LESSON

8 A Return Expedition: Working as Researchers

MATERIALS

- Student journals
- Access to library
- Handout 3.1: Big6 Research Handbook
- Handout 8.1: Nonfiction Text Evaluation Form
- Appendix A2: Big6 Research Process Poster (displayed in the classroom)

Research is an organized and systematic way of finding answers to questions.

OBJECTIVES

Students will:

- locate and access various library materials.

SEQUENCE

WARM UP

1. Say: *Yesterday, we went to the library and you began locating and accessing sources to help you answer your research question. Take a few minutes to write about this experience in your journal. Consider these questions:*
   - Did you learn any important research tips that you could share with your fellow researchers?
   - When you go back to the library today, what is your plan of attack?

- Give students about 5–7 minutes to write.
- Allow another 5–10 minutes for students to share their responses.

- For those students who struggle in written expression, consider discussing these questions orally.
- Read students' journal entries before the next lesson. It will give you information that you will not be able to visually observe. Do your best to get a good idea of the progress each child is making. One day a child may be a very successful researcher and the next he or she could become very frustrated. It will also give you a good idea of students you could pair to conduct research together. For example:
  - Pair a student who is having success locating and accessing information with a student who is struggling.
  - Pair two students with similar research questions.
  - Pair strong researchers to work in independent teams and create a small group of struggling researchers for you and another small group for the librarian.

INSTRUCTION: RESEARCH REVIEW

2. Review the concept of *research* and the research process. Talk with the students about how research is a process and the researcher will often spend days, weeks, months, and even years researching a question. It all depends on the amount of existing information on a particular topic.

Share with the students that some of them have topics that lots and lots of people have written about and have extensively researched— they will find what seems like endless resources. Others, however, have much narrower topics that few people have written about and/or researched. This may require them to dig deeper and dig often.

3. Explain to the students that they (and you, too) are going back to the library to RE-search, to search again. Researchers like historians, scientists, teachers, mathematicians, etc., have a plan for their research.

Discuss with students what might happen if researchers began researching without a plan. Ask: *What if we go into the library today without an understanding of the Big6 process and without specific daily goals? What do you think would happen to our research?* Guide students to recognize that they could do myriad things: (1) wander around and never find valuable sources, (2) get caught up in one text, (3) read without a purpose, etc.

4. Help students determine which step of the Big6 research process they have accomplished, and help them determine their research goals for today. Explain that because they are all different people and all have different research questions, they may be on different steps and have different goals. However, it is still early in the research process and they may still be working on accomplishing the same tasks.

- Refer to the Big6 poster (Appendix A2) in the classroom and ask: *Do we all know what our task is? Who can define the task?*
- Call on a student who will either paraphrase the task or read it verbatim from his or her Big6 Research Handbook.
- Pose questions like: *Who would like to share their question? Have we determined all of the possible sources we can access to find answers to our questions and what are some of those sources? Will we all access the same types of sources? Why or why not?*
- Think aloud: *So the way I see it is we know our task and we know what kinds of sources we need to seek to complete our task. Is it safe to say that now we are all locating and accessing sources? Good. Tomorrow we are going to talk about how to use the information we find.*

5. Distribute Handout 8.1: Nonfiction Text Evaluation Form. Explain to students that today when they find a book, they need to critically analyze the value of the book.

Ask students to share in what ways could a book on their topic *not* be helpful to their research. Examples may include:

- Too hard to read
- Too outdated
- Not written by an expert in the field
- Seems to contain wrong information

If your library does not have current books on a student's research topic, they may have to use literature that is outdated. Keep this is mind when explaining the copyright date and what it means for a student's research.

6. Model filling out Handout 8.1 on the smartboard/overhead, using a book from the Explorer's Cart. Ask if there are questions. Make sure students know how to locate the information for this form. Your modeling should cover this. Tell students they are required to fill out one of these forms today in the library, but they should always think about these questions as they select sources. If time allows, give students an opportunity to practice with a book from the cart prior to evaluating their own sources.

ACTIVITY: LIBRARY VISIT

7. Review today's library goals. Students will:
   - evaluate a selected nonfiction text and turn in the evaluation form when it is complete, and
   - select a book to check out and keep in the classroom, and find a helpful reference text to keep on the Reference Cart.

- Use the completed evaluation forms as informal assessment and monitor student progress and understanding.
- Make sure you schedule the library visit ahead of time. If possible, make sure the librarian is available to assist students.

8. Ask: *Any questions? Concerns? Comments?* Instruct students to work independently in the library.

CLOSE

9. Ask: *Now that you've had a chance to work as researchers, what do you think are some qualities a good researcher must have? Why? Create a class list that can be posted and added to throughout the unit.*

PREPARATION: FOR NEXT LESSON

10. During the next lesson, students will be grouped in small groups of 3–4 for an activity in which they discuss a journal prompt. Group students together who appear to have a similar capacity for high level, conceptual thinking in relation to the unit content. Determine these groups in advance by using your anecdotal records from research observations and journal entries.
11. Select a passage from a text you are using for your research and copy it onto an overhead (or smartboard, etc.) before the next lesson. Pick a short passage to use for a model lesson. Be sure you fully review Lesson 9 in its entirety to understand what you will be doing with this passage.

HANDOUT 8.1

NONFICTION TEXT EVALUATION FORM

Title of book: ______________________

Author: ______________________

1. Is the text readable for YOU? ❑ YES ❑ NO

2. What is the copyright date? (**Hint:** Look on the back of the title page.) ____________

   Because of the copyright date, do you think this text contains useful and/or current information about your topic? ❑ YES ❑ NO

3. Are there pictures or diagrams in this book? ❑ YES ❑ NO

   If so, are they helpful to you? ❑ YES ❑ NO

- -

NONFICTION TEXT EVALUATION FORM

Title of book: ______________________

Author: ______________________

1. Is the text readable for YOU? ❑ YES ❑ NO

2. What is the copyright date? (**Hint:** Look on the back of the title page.) ____________

   Because of the copyright date, do you think this text contains useful and/or current information about your topic? ❑ YES ❑ NO

3. Are there pictures or diagrams in this book? ❑ YES ❑ NO

   If so, are they helpful to you? ❑ YES ❑ NO

LESSON

9 Working as Researchers: Exploring Texts and Organizing Ideas

Teacher's Note: This lesson may take longer than 45 minutes. You may choose to break this lesson into two separate sessions. A good stopping point for the first session is noted in the lesson plan.

MATERIALS

- ✓ Student journals
- ✓ Dictionary definition of the words *plagiarism* and *paraphrase*
- ✓ Library books from the Explorer's Cart
- ✓ Access to the library
- ✓ Sample text (see Preparation section in Lesson 8)
- ✓ Handout 9.1: Plagiarism Scenarios (cut into strips)
- ✓ Handout 9.2: Researcher's Notebook

Research is an organized and systematic way of finding answers to questions.

OBJECTIVES

Students will:

- ✓ define plagiarism and describe its consequences,
- ✓ collect and analyze information relevant to the topic/question, and
- ✓ read a passage and paraphrase what was read (note-taking system).

- Plagiarism
- Paraphrasing

SEQUENCE

WARM UP

- Pay close attention to students who are writing their responses and substituting the idea of "correct" for "right" and "incorrect" for "wrong." Gently guide the student to the idea of morally right with age-appropriate examples.
- Give students time to adequately respond to the prompt.

1. Ask students to respond to the following prompt in their journals: *What is the difference between right and wrong? How do you know when you or someone else is right, and how do you know when you or someone else is wrong?*
2. Place students in groups of 3–4. Have them discuss their answers to the prompt. As students discuss, closely monitor their conversations. Provide them with probing questions if you find that they finish sharing early. Ask them questions like:
   - ✓ Did you all write the same kind of answer to the question?
   - ✓ Do you all agree?
   - ✓ Why might people have different answers?

Keep students in these groups; do not send them back to home base.

Determine small groups of 3–4 in advance by using formative assessment responses, as well as your anecdotal records from research observations and past journal entries (see Preparation section in Lesson 8).

INSTRUCTION: DISCUSSING PLAGIARISM

- Before teaching the plagiarism lesson, review: http://www.indiana.edu/~wts/pamphlets/plagiarism.shtml#original.
- Ensure that you are clear about the definition of *plagiarism* as it relates to academic work including research reports.

3. Explain to students that today you are going to talk about a topic that is very controversial in the research world. And it's very important that researchers understand this concept! Write the word *plagiarism* on the board. Ask students to quietly sound it out and to determine if (and where) they have heard this word before.
4. Put the dictionary definition of plagiarism on the overhead/board. Talk about the pronunciation of the word and its definition. Include the word origin: The word *plagiarism* comes from the Latin word *plagiarius* (pronounced plah-ghee-AR-ee-us), which means *kidnapper*.
5. Ask: *How is plagiarism like kidnapping? How can plagiarism affect your research?* Discuss why it is unethical. Make sure students have a strong grasp of what it means to plagiarize.

ACTIVITY: PLAGIARISM SCENARIOS

6. Distribute Handout 9.1: Plagiarism Scenarios strips to groups. Explain to students that they are now going to read about the work of some other students. In their groups, instruct students to:

- ✓ read the scenario silently,
- ✓ pick someone to read the scenario aloud, and
- ✓ discuss if they think the researcher plagiarized or did not plagiarize.

Difficulty levels of plagiarism scenarios:

- Eric: Very Difficult
- Sara: Difficult
- Brian: Medium
- Jamie: Easy
- Adam: Very Easy

Make sure you give one scenario slip to each student so they can read silently and be able to refer back to the text during discussion. Walk around as students read and discuss the scenarios. If a group finishes early, give them another scenario slip to analyze.

7. Reassemble the class. Place each scenario one at a time on the overhead projector (or smartboard, etc.) and have students talk about the plagiarism that they found in that particular researcher's work. Start with Adam and work back to Eric.

Teacher's Note: This is a natural break in the lesson. If time is a concern, stop here and continue next class.

INSTRUCTION: USE OF INFORMATION

8. Ask: *How do you suppose we make sure that **we** don't plagiarize as we collect and report about **our** research? The best way to avoid plagiarism is to make sure we take our **own notes**, in our **own words**. Today, I'm going to show you how to do that.*
9. Distribute Handout 9.2: Researcher's Notebook. Tell students that you are going to model the note-taking system they are going to use to collect their research. Instruct students to look at the Note Card sheets in the Researcher's Notebook. Ask them to tell you what they notice about the pages in the Notebook. You want students talking about the source list on the left and the INSERT notations. Briefly review the INSERT strategy from Lesson 7.

If you feel the INSERT notation system is too much to incorporate with the note-taking instruction at this time, you may omit that and have the students ignore those symbols.

You will need to support many students when they start taking notes for the first time. Try to get some extra hands in the classroom for this lesson.

10. Put a passage from your research up on the overhead. Tell students it is a passage from a text that you are researching for your project on the discovery of America. This passage has a lot of important information, but you have to be very careful that you do not use the same words as this author. Share that sometimes this is difficult, because in many cases you might feel that the author says it better than you ever could. But you know it is wrong to plagiarize, so you must take notes with **your** words. Say: *When we put what we write into our **own** words, we are avoiding plagiarizing. Paraphrasing is a way to make sure we aren't plagiarizing.*
11. Point out that Step 4 in the Big6 deals with using information—how to get it from a source and record it. Note taking helps with this step.
12. Model the note-taking system. Have your Researcher's Notebook open and instruct students to have theirs open as well. Read a portion of the text (that is up on the overhead), then cover it with another sheet so it is not visible to you or the students. Restate what you just read in your own words.

- This is very important for the students to see and understand why you do this. After you have restated what you just read, move to the note card. Write the salient points of your restatement or write your restatement in its entirety. When you have finished that, go back to the source list (on the note card) and circle what kind of source you just accessed.
- Next, look at the book and write down the title and author on the Source lines of the note card. Finally, think aloud about what kind of information you just recorded: *Does it fit an INSERT category? What is something you knew (check mark)? An important idea (plus sign)? A wow statement (exclamation point)? Something you don't understand (a question mark)? Or something you'd like to go back to (an asterisk)?* Circle the INSERT notation mark if it fits in one of those categories.

13. Model through a Think Aloud: *I think I am going to read more from this passage. It has a lot of important information. Now I move to Note Card 2, because I want to put only one piece of information on each note card. This will help me organize my ideas later. Okay, the top portion of Note Card 2 is really easy to fill out. I get to circle the exact same source type on the top left. I am just going to copy the exact same information for the source line as I did in Note Card 1. Now I am going to read the next chunk of text. Perhaps the next paragraph will be a good chunk of text.*
14. Read the paragraph aloud; allow students to view it on the overhead.
15. Continue with the think aloud: *Okay, I am going to cover the passage up so I am not tempted to copy it word for word, because that could lead to plagiarism and I don't want to do that! Now, let's think, what did I just read about? Paraphrase aloud what you've read. Fill out Note Card 2 accordingly.*

16. Ask: *Now for Note Card 3, I decided to access and read a newspaper article. How would the top of Note Card 3 look different than Note Cards 1 and 2?*
17. Share with students that in this lesson you have been doing something called paraphrasing. Write the word *paraphrase* on the board. Ask: *Any idea what it means to paraphrase? Think about what you just watched me do.* Talk about the word and use it in sentences. Ensure that students become familiar with the word.

You may explain to them that in some research papers, direct quotes are used. For this research project, however, students will be paraphrasing.

- *Paraphrase* (noun, verb, -phrased, -phras•ing.): (1) a restatement of a text or passage giving the meaning in another form, as for clearness; rewording. (2) the act or process of restating or rewording
  - *Note:* The prefix *para* is from Greek and means "beside" or "by;" this original use was extended such that para became attached to words to mean "auxiliary to" or "derivative of," or "abnormal" or "less than."
  - *Phrase* comes from "phrazien," which means "to tell."
  - Paraphrase means to tell in other words, or in a way that is near to or derivative from the original text, to achieve clarity.

18. Instruct students that it is now their turn to use the note-taking strategy and to paraphrase what they've read. Everyone should have a Researcher's Notebook with their name on it. Everyone should also have multiple Note Card Sheets in their Researcher's Notebook. Check for this. Tell students that they may use a source from the library, or a source from the Explorer's Cart, to practice their note-taking techniques. Ask if there are any questions before taking students to the library.
19. At the library, students should engage in independent research and note taking.

PREPARATION: FORMATIVE ASSESSMENT 4

Check for understanding of plagiarism by asking students to respond to the following questions in their journals or as an exit card:

1. Define plagiarism.
2. What do you think might cause a researcher to plagiarize?
3. Imagine that you have been asked to explain paraphrasing to a group of other fifth graders. What will you tell them?

4. Use paraphrasing to convey the meaning of this sentence: Bill Gates knew so much about computers as a youngster that his school had him design a program that would help figure out student class schedules.

HANDOUT 9.1

PLAGIARISM SCENARIOS

SARA

When taking notes for her research report, Sara copies the words directly from the books and websites she accesses. When she sits down to write her report, she plans to change the notes into her own words.

ERIC

Eric reads a report by a famous scientist. The scientist explains a new theory about birds and migration. Eric writes his report about birds and titles the report, "My Thoughts About Birds and Migration: A New Theory."

BRIAN

Brian has to write a paragraph about dinosaurs. He finds a great paragraph in an encyclopedia. He copies the paragraph in his own handwriting and rewrites the first and last sentence of the paragraph in his own words.

JAMIE

Jamie's teacher assigns her to do a report on polar bears. Jamie finds a great website on these large animals. She copies a portion of the website text and pastes it into her report. She finishes the report with a paragraph of her own words.

ADAM

Adam had baseball practice and could not finish his social studies homework. Kris offers to help Adam and emails his homework to Adam. Adam prints it out and puts his name on the top. He hands it to his teacher first thing in the morning.

HANDOUT 9.2

RESEARCHER'S NOTEBOOK

Research Question: ______

Encyclopedia Website Magazine Newspaper Nonfiction text Personal interview Other: ______	Date: ______ **Source:** Title: ______ ______ Author: ______

INSERT Strategy

✓ + ! ? *

______

______

______

______

______

______

______

______

______

______

______

LESSON

10 Working as Researchers: Reexploring Texts and Reorganizing Ideas

MATERIALS

- ✓ Index cards (one per student)
- ✓ Student research portfolios
- ✓ Access to the library
- ✓ Handout 9.2: Researcher's Notebook
- ✓ Appendix A6: Anecdotal Record Form

Research is an organized and systematic way of finding answers to questions.

OBJECTIVES

Students will:

- ✓ locate and access various library materials, and
- ✓ identify an area for improvement.

SEQUENCE

WARM UP

1. Distribute an index card to each student. Remind students that yesterday they worked with paraphrasing and Note Card Sheets in their Researcher's Notebooks. Ask them to think about their experience yesterday. What was difficult for them? Where did they struggle? Assure them that it is normal to have some difficulty and they will continue to have some difficulty, because researching like this is a new skill for them.

- You can use this index card strategy in other lessons, even if it isn't listed in the lesson plan.
- As soon as you get students settled in the library, quickly read over the index cards. Meet first with the students who seem to be having the most difficultly just getting started.

On one side of the index card, ask the students to write about what is difficult for them in this research process. On the other side of the card, ask them to write their independent research goal for today.

2. Collect index cards. Tell students that they will soon learn, if they haven't already, that researching requires patience, dedication, and perseverance. They will have to tackle their research questions over and over again, until they are sure they have uncovered enough quality information to successfully address the questions.

ACTIVITY: LIBRARY TIME

3. Tell students that in the library during this lesson they will:
   - ✓ research independently, and
   - ✓ meet with you for researcher-teacher conferences.

During independent research time in the library, you will have to meet with students on a one-on-one basis to make sure they are making progress. You will want to record the "happenings" in these short conferences on Appendix A6: Anecdotal Record Form.

CLOSE

4. Ask students: *Did you meet your goals for today? Why or why not? What qualities would you like to add to our class list of the qualities of good researchers? Why?*

PREPARATION: FOR NEXT LESSON

5. The contents of the research portfolio up to this point are:
   - ✓ Handout 1.3: Anticipation Guide (returned with comments)
   - ✓ Handout 3.1: Big6 Research Handbook
   - ✓ Handout 4.2: KWL Chart
   - ✓ Handout 8.1: Nonfiction Text Evaluation Form (returned with comments)
   - ✓ Handout 9.2: Researcher's Notebook
   - ✓ Materials the researcher added that are pertinent to his or her research question

As you review the students' research portfolios, you will most likely find that some students are struggling with putting information in their own words. Conduct mini-lessons on paraphrasing with small groups of students as needed. First, read aloud a piece of nonfiction text. Then, have the students try to rephrase the text in only 2–3 sentences. Repeat as needed.

LESSON

11 Researchers as Project Designers

MATERIALS

- ✓ Student research portfolios
- ✓ Access to the library
- ✓ Handout 11.1: Researcher's Contract

Research is an organized and systematic way of finding answers to questions.

OBJECTIVES

Students will:

- ✓ determine effective methods to communicate research findings, and
- ✓ determine incremental benchmarks to reach a goal.

SEQUENCE

WARM UP

1. Talk with students about the main big idea of this unit: Research is an organized and systematic way of finding answers to questions.

Engage students in a discussion about how that big idea works with the steps in the Big6 research process. Next, generally review the Big6 process. Ask: *What have we completed or almost completed in this process?*

- Task Definition
- Information Seeking Strategies
- Location and Access
- Use of Information

Make sure students are keeping all of their research resources (handbook, notebook, etc.) in their research portfolio. You will need to access these to determine students' progress. (See Preparation section in Lesson 10 for portfolio contents.)

Instruct students to talk briefly about the first four steps. Ask: *What does each step entail? Do they find it an easy step or a more difficult one?*

2. Talk about the next step in the Big6 process—Step 5: Synthesis. Ask if anyone has ideas about what *synthesis* means or what they are going to be doing during this step of the process. Solicit answers and then dissect the word *synthesis*.

- *Synthesis* (noun): the combining of separate elements to form a whole
  - *Note:* The prefix *syn* is from Greek and means "to put."
  - *Thesis* is the central idea in a piece of writing that the writer wants to prove.

- Listen to other product variations students may suggest. In the end, you decide if the presentation format they choose is acceptable.
- If your students have not yet worked with PowerPoint, you will either want to give a lesson on how to create an effective presentation, or omit this as an option all together.
- Dioramas are not recommended for this project as they do not allow students to demonstrate in-depth analysis of their research questions.

INSTRUCTION: INDEPENDENT RESEARCH CONTRACT

3. Tell students that today they have a very big decision to make. They must determine the best way to synthesize and share their research findings with an audience.

Within 2 weeks (you can be more exact when you've set the gala date), students will present their research findings to a real audience. This audience will be made up of different adults in their community. (If you see panic in their eyes, reassure them that they will be more than prepared for this event.)

4. Explain to the students that before you talk in greater detail about the Research Gala, they each need to individually determine the way they want to synthesize and present their research. Briefly highlight three different presentation styles they can chose from.

- **Paper:** You can write a paper. This is the most popular research presentation style of professional researchers. The paper will be approximately 3, typed pages in length.
- **Presentation:** You can create a visual presentation. This would come in the form of a trifold board, PowerPoint presentation, documentary (video), or another form we discuss.
- **Performance:** This is for the creative thinkers who will take on a role other than self. The researcher using this format may create a song, come dressed as a character and present the information as that character, or another form we discuss.

Meet with each student individually and talk about his or her Researcher's Contract. When all of the necessary steps are in place, both of you sign the contract. Have students take the contract home to be signed by a parent or guardian.

5. Give students time to ask questions and think about these choices.
6. Distribute Handout 11.1: Researcher's Contract. Talk with students about the purpose of this contract and how it is a document to help

them stay on track. You can also talk about how researchers in the field often have formal or informal contracts with publishers, and that keeping on track to reach a deadline is a skill that many researchers struggle with. Fill in the common portions of this document: Name, question, product choice, gala date, and preparation for gala dates.

ACTIVITY: INDEPENDENT RESEARCH

7. Tell students that for the rest of class today, they will continue conducting research in the library. As they are researching, you are going to sit down with each one of them and talk about their research contract. These contracts are due back to you tomorrow. Explain to the children that they will have to go home tonight and determine exactly what needs to get done from now until the research gala for them to be a successful researcher. Suggestion: Write in pencil!
8. Ask if there are questions.
9. Head to the library for independent research time and researcher-teacher conferences.

If you have sufficient resources in the classroom at this point, you might choose to facilitate independent research time in the classroom rather than in the library.

HOMEWORK

10. Remind students to take home the Researcher's Contract (Handout 11.1) and have it signed by a parent or guardian.

PREPARATION: FOR NEXT LESSON

11. Researcher's Contracts will be collected at the beginning of the next lesson. Look through these to ensure students have covered all appropriate steps before Lesson 12.
12. Once students have selected their presentation products, make time to meet with them in small groups to discuss how to create high-quality products. For example, all students who decide to create a PowerPoint presentation should discuss with you the qualities of an engaging and informative PowerPoint. Specifically, how many slides might be too many or too few? You may find it necessary to base these lessons on students' readiness levels to ensure that the highest-end learners are challenged by differentiated product requirements. Such mini-lessons can be held over the next few lessons.

HANDOUT 11.1

RESEARCHER'S CONTRACT

Research Question: ______________________________

Product Choice: ❑ paper ❑ presentation ❑ performance

In the next _______ days I will complete my independent research as well as my method for sharing my findings. I realize this will require me to work at home each evening in addition to the work I do during the school day. I understand that fulfilling this contract will take a lot of organization, self-reliance, and responsibility. I agree to ask for help from my teacher, librarian, and parent when I am not sure of what to do or if I feel I am not making sufficient progress.

Below is my detailed plan for the next _______ days.

Day	Goals for the Day	Self-Check	Adult-Check
	• RESEARCH GALA!		

Student Signature: ______________________________ Date: ______________

Teacher Signature: ______________________________ Date: ______________

Parent or Guardian Signature: ______________________ Date: ______________

LESSON

12 Researchers as Presenters

MATERIALS

- ✓ Student research portfolios
- ✓ Access to the library or Explorer's Cart
- ✓ Handout 12.1: Do and Don't Chart
- ✓ Handout 12.2: Research Gala Product Rubric
- ✓ Appendix A7: Teacher Script for Mock Presentation/Evaluation Session

Research is an organized and systematic way of finding answers to questions.

OBJECTIVES

Students will:

- ✓ determine a set of criteria on which to judge quality research and
- ✓ conduct independent research.

SEQUENCE

WARM UP

1. Collect Handout 11.1: Researcher's Contract.
2. Talk with students about the fact that a researcher doesn't only look up information; he or she is also a project designer. Tell students that in addition to designing their project, they will stand next to it and answer questions about it.

Explain that at the Research Gala (Lesson 15) they all will have their own area to set up. Some will have a paper and the Research Notebook; others will have computers, trifold boards, etc.

Appendix A7 provides a sample script about puppy care. However, you may change these presentations to "Who Really Discovered America?" based on the research you have collected.

INSTRUCTION: PRESENTATION STYLES

3. Tell students you are going to present to them information on research. Explain that you will give two presentations. Encourage students to pay attention to the differences and let them know you will discuss them as a class when you are finished. Present your findings.

ACTIVITY: SMALL GROUP DISCUSSION

4. Display the following questions/prompts on the overhead, board, or smartboard for small groups to discuss.

- What could I improve on for my first presentation?
- Make a list of characteristics of a successful presenter.
- If you had to judge your classmates presentation, what would you want to see and hear? Make a list of possible project requirements for your classmates

Possible Presenter Characteristics:

- Organized
- Neatly dressed
- Can easily explain his or her research
- Comfortable and confident
- Can answer questions about his or her research

Possible Evaluation Criteria:

- Stuck to research question
- Used various sources
- Used a note-taking system
- Product is well organized
- Can easily explain research

5. When the students have had enough time to discuss (or you feel they are struggling with the tasks), move back to a whole-class group. Share ideas.
6. Distribute Handout 12.1: Do and Don't Chart. Based on the ideas generated by the questions, complete the chart and have students keep these in their research portfolios. This chart should help aid the students in preparing their presentation.
7. Distribute Handout 12.2: Research Gala Product Rubric. Tell students that this is the form you will use to assess when they see you during the Research Gala. Explain that you are giving this to them ahead of time so they know exactly what you will be looking for. There will be no surprises. Everything is right here on this form. Carefully review the Research Gala Product Rubric with the students. Ask and answer questions. Tell them to keep this form in their research portfolios as they prepare for the gala.

ACTIVITY: LIBRARY

8. Head to the library for independent research time and researcher-teacher conferences.

If you have sufficient resources in the classroom at this point, you might choose to facilitate independent research time in the classroom rather than the library.

HANDOUT 12.1

DO AND DON'T CHART

WHEN PRESENTING YOUR RESEARCH	
DO	DON'T

Name: ________________________________ Date: ______________

HANDOUT 12.2

RESEARCH GALA PRODUCT RUBRIC

Researcher's Name:
Project Title/Question:

Product Format: ❑ paper ❑ presentation ❑ performance

Criteria	Yes	No
Task Definition		
Researcher developed a research question		
Findings answer posed research question		
Information Seeking Strategies		
Researcher used 3 or more sources to answer question		
Location and Access		
Researcher used different resources (websites, nonfiction books, magazines, etc.)		
Use of Information		
Researcher's Notebook accompanies project		
Researcher used a note-taking system		
Researcher kept track of sources		
Researcher paraphrased correct facts on note cards		
Synthesis		
Researcher presented relevant and important information		
Researcher could answer questions about project		
Evaluation		
Researcher could explain what he or she would do differently next time		

Comments: ______________________________

____

____

____

____

____

____

LESSON 13 Preparation for Gala

Teacher's Note: Depending upon where your students are in the research process, you may need multiple independent research sessions.

MATERIALS

- ✓ Index cards (one per student, if you choose to begin the lesson with the optional warm-up activity that was used in Lesson 10)
- ✓ Access to library or Explorer's Cart
- ✓ Handout 11.1: Researcher's Contract
- ✓ Handout 12.2: Research Gala Product Rubric

Research is an organized and systematic way of finding answers to questions.

OBJECTIVES

Students will:

- ✓ synthesize multiple sources of information.

INDEPENDENT RESEARCH SESSION

1. Today you will support students as they prepare for the Research Gala. Some points to consider:
   - ✓ You may want to begin with the index card warm-up used in Lesson 10.
   - ✓ You may want to station the librarian in the library while you work in the classroom. This way, students who require additional research time can go to the library while students who are already synthesizing information into their presentation can remain in the classroom.

- ✓ Having extra hands in the classroom or the library will be helpful. However, if parents volunteer, you may want to request that they not work with their own children.

2. Remind students to consistently consult the rubric and their Researcher's Contract to make sure they are on track to produce high quality work.
3. Leave some time at the end to answer final questions before the gala. Also discuss proper dress for the gala if you want your students to dress like "professional researchers." You should be explicit with your students if they will be expected to wear particular attire (for example, no shorts or t-shirts). Finally, ask students:
   - ✓ What were some things the researchers did to effectively present their work?
   - ✓ What do you think you can do to make your presentation the best it can be?

LESSON

14 Preparation for Gala: The Dress Rehearsal

MATERIALS

- ✓ Handout 12.1: Do and Don't Chart

OBJECTIVES

Students will:

- ✓ participate in a mock Research Gala, and
- ✓ present a synthesis of various sources.

SEQUENCE

1. During this lesson, provide students with the opportunity to practice for the gala. Some points to consider:
   - ✓ Either have students present one at a time in the front of the class or set up "mini gala" locations throughout the classroom.
   - ✓ If you decide to set up mini galas, have half of the class members stand with their projects and research portfolios while the other half rotates and asks questions.
   - ✓ Review Handout 12.1 for presenting your research.
   - ✓ Switch roles halfway through the lesson.

2. Leave some time at the end to answer final questions about the gala. Remind students of appropriate dress for the gala.

HOMEWORK

3. For homework, or in class after the dress rehearsal, have students complete Handout 4.1: KWL Chart (L column) and Handout 12.2: Research Gala Product Rubric.

LESSON

15 Research Gala

MATERIALS

- ✓ Student research portfolios
- ✓ Refreshments
- ✓ Name tags
- ✓ Handout 12.2: Research Gala Product Rubric (teacher copies)
- ✓ Handout 15.1: Unit Reflection Form
- ✓ Handout 15.2: Performance Assessment
- ✓ Handout 15.3: Performance Assessment Rubric (teacher copies)
- ✓ Appendix A8: Sample Letter

- The contributions of an explorer's journey can be analyzed from various perspectives.
- Research is an organized and systematic way of finding answers to questions.

OBJECTIVES

Students will:

- ✓ present original research to an audience.

SEQUENCE

1. Today is the day! Make sure each student knows where to set up his or her work. During the gala, when students are not formally presenting their research, they should be seated and listening to the research presentations of their classmates.
2. **Summative Assessment:** As students present their research, use the Research Gala Product Rubric (Handout 12.2) to assess each student.

HOMEWORK

3. After all students have presented their research, have students complete Handout 15.1: Unit Reflection Form.

PREPARATION: PERFORMANCE ASSESSMENT

4. Administer the Unit 1 Performance Assessment (Handout 15.2) during the next lesson or soon after the research gala. You will need to provide students 60 minutes to complete the assessment. Read the instructions aloud first to the students, then read the letter from Dr. Dugan. Emphasize the bulleted points in the letter. Use the Unit 1 Performance Assessment Rubric (Handout 15.3) to score each student as expert, apprentice, or novice. You may compare student responses to the sample letter provided (Appendix A8) to assist in scoring. Share the completed rubric with the students.

HANDOUT 15.1

UNIT REFLECTION FORM

EXPLORATION

Name: ______________________

Date: ______________________

UNIT REFLECTION ASSIGNMENT

1. What did you like most about this unit of study? Why?

2. If you were given the chance to go back and re-research your question, what would you do differently the second time around?

These things came easily for me:	These things were difficult for me:

HANDOUT 15.2

PERFORMANCE ASSESSMENT

A LETTER FROM THE EXPERT

Directions: You, the expert researcher, will demonstrate your understanding of the research process by writing a letter. You will read a letter from Dr. Dugan, consider her request, and respond by writing your own letter back to her on a separate sheet of paper. You must complete this task within an hour and work independently.

Dr. Donna Dugan
Hainesville College
Department of History
111 College Circle
Collegeville, NE

Dear Researcher,

Good day, I hope this letter finds you well.

My purpose for this letter is to ask for your help. I will soon begin conducting research for my book, *America's Most Influential People of Past and Present*. As you may realize, this will be quite a big job! Because my expertise is in writing and not researching, I have hit a bit of a snag.

I do not have a clear plan of action to effectively find answers to my question, and that is why I am writing to you. I know two things:

- My research question: Who is the most influential American of all time? (I will rank the top 100 I uncover.)
- Research is an organized and systematic way of finding answers to questions.

However, I am unsure of an effective process to systematically conduct this research investigation. I am asking you to take a few minutes out of your busy schedule to write me a letter that details a process you would use to answer this research question.

Areas I would like you to consider:

- Particular steps to answering a research questions
- Effective research strategies for each step

HANDOUT 15.2, CONTINUED

> - Reading strategies I can use for effective comprehension and organization of nonfiction material
>
> Thank you in advance for your time.
>
> Sincerely,
>
> Donna Dugan, Ph.D.

RESPONSE HELPER

- ✓ **Format:** Business letter
- ✓ **Audience:** Dr. Dugan
- ✓ **Topic:** An effective research process
- ✓ **Purpose:** To provide Dr. Dugan with a step-by-step process to effectively conduct research

HANDOUT 15.3

PERFORMANCE ASSESSMENT RUBRIC

Criteria	Expert	Apprentice	Novice
Process in General	Articulates a clear and comprehensive understanding of the multiple steps required to conduct an effective research investigation—as evidenced by the presence of all six steps of the Big6 process.	Provides an adequate understanding of the multiple steps required to conduct an effective research investigation—as evidenced by including most of the steps in the Big6 process.	Shows a minimal understanding of the multiple steps required to conduct an effective research investigation—as evidenced by only including three or fewer steps in the Big6 process.
Application to Context	The quality of the product reflects the researcher's ability to effectively apply a research process to the context provided—as evidenced by multiple connections between the steps of the Big6 process and the topic of influential Americans.	Adequate considerations and references are made to the implementation of an effective process in the context provided.	Inability to connect the research process to this particular context; the "influential Americans" context is rarely if ever mentioned in the letter.
Reading and Research Strategies	Articulately explains the implementation and relevance of multiple reading and research strategies; these strategies are accurately and seamlessly integrated into the process and careful consideration of the context is evident.	Adequately explains the implementation of multiple reading and research strategies; most strategies are accurately integrated into the process.	Letter contains few to no reading or research strategies or the explanation of the strategies contains incorrect information.

Unit 2
Aristotle's Rhetoric
Learning the Art of Persuasion

BACKGROUND

Aristotle's Rhetoric: Learning the Art of Persuasion is designed to help students develop the ability to persuade others as they expand their writing, reading, listening, and oral advocacy skills. The ancient Greek philosopher Aristotle described rhetoric as "the faculty of observing in any given case the available means of persuasion." He was referring to the way a speaker uses specific modes of appealing to a particular audience, or appeals, in order to persuade its members to do or believe something. The use of appeals, including ethos, pathos, and logos, by contemporary advocates is essential to persuading an audience. Thus, the title of the unit, Aristotle's Rhetoric: Learning the Art of Persuasion, reflects one of the big ideas of rhetoric: Rhetoric is an art that can be studied systematically.

The activities and assessment products in this unit encourage students to develop their persuasive writing skills in conjunction with their ability to evaluate the written and spoken efforts to persuade made by others. In addition, this unit builds upon skills and strategies taught in other CLEAR Curriculum units thus giving students multiple opportunities to deepen their capacities as articulate, observant, and convincing oral advocates. All students will have opportunities to read, listen to, and critically examine a range of rhetorical samples—

speeches, commercials, political advertisements, eulogies, and more—believed by experts in the field of rhetoric to be exemplary in their ability to persuade an audience. The unit also gives students many opportunities for engaging in argument relevant to their own interests and experiences that will enhance their writing and oral advocacy skills. All of the activities are developed in correspondence with and are extensions of state and national standards including the Common Core State Standards (CCSS). By the end of the unit, each student will have designed, researched, and delivered a complete rhetorical endeavor, which they will share with an audience consisting of students, parents, and teachers at a classroom Ode to Aristotle Rhetoric Gala.

OBJECTIVES/STANDARDS

Aristotle's Rhetoric: Learning the Art of Persuasion aligns with common state fifth-grade reading and writing standards and national standards outlined by the National Council of Teachers of English (NCTE). It also reflects fifth and sixth grade reading, writing, and speaking and listening standards in the CCSS, including those specifically addressing the development of oral advocacy skills (an alignment chart is provided on p. 265). This unit addresses the following objectives:

STUDENTS WILL KNOW THE FOLLOWING TERMS

- *Rhetoric* is the verbalization of ideas that persuade others to do or believe something. Per Aristotle, rhetoric involves the "faculty of observing in any given case the available means of persuasion," including ethos, pathos, and logos.
- *Ethos* is an appeal to the credibility or authority of the speaker; ethos requires that the speaker be trustworthy and of high moral character.
- *Pathos* is an appeal to the emotions of the audience members.
- *Logos* is an appeal to logic and reason.
- *Appeal* is a term referring to the three modes of persuasion, specifically ethos, pathos, and logos.
- *Syllogism* is a logical argument that has a major premise ("all men are mortal"), a minor premise ("Socrates is a man"), and an inevitable conclusion ("Socrates is mortal").
- *Logical fallacy* is an argument that uses poor reasoning.
- *Ad hominem* is an argument that attacks the credibility (or ethos) of a speaker.
- *Anaphora* is the repetition of a word or phrase at the beginning of successive phrases, clauses, or lines.

- *Antithesis* is the opposition or juxtaposition of ideas or words in a balanced or parallel construction.
- *Conduplicato* is the repetition of a word or phrase within successive phrases, clauses, or lines. Also called parallelism.
- *Deliberative rhetoric* is prepared speech that is designed to convince an audience based on facts and logic. Also called political rhetoric.
- *Enthymeme* is a syllogism with a conclusion so obvious that the major and minor premises need not be stated.
- *Epideictic rhetoric* is prepared speech that is designed to inspire and unify an audience.
- *Euphemism* is a substitution of a more pleasant expression for one whose meaning may come across as sad, rude, or offensive.
- *Forensic rhetoric* is prepared speech that is designed to convince an audience of what happened and what to do about it.
- *Hyperbole* is exaggeration for emphasis or for rhetorical effect.
- *Paralipsis* is pretending to omit something by drawing attention to it.
- *Rhetorical question* is a question that is posed for emphasis rather than for the purpose of getting an answer.

STUDENTS WILL UNDERSTAND THE FOLLOWING BIG IDEAS ABOUT RHETORIC

- Rhetoric is an art that can be studied systematically.
- Rhetoric serves as a call to action.
- Rhetoricians use a variety of appeals to persuade an audience to do or believe something.
- Understanding the interests and values of an audience is key to persuasion.
- Statements that are true and logical have a natural tendency to prevail over their opposites.
- The use of logic and reason, rather than force, to persuade others to do or believe something is a uniquely human capacity.
- Rhetoric is vital to a healthy democracy.
- The ability to evaluate rhetoric used by others is critical to making informed decisions.
- Rhetoric can be used to promote or injure the common good.

STUDENTS WILL DEMONSTRATE THE FOLLOWING SKILLS

- Generate ideas for persuasive writing.
- Build rhetoric vocabulary.
- Identify the values and interests of the audience.

- Use clear reasons and relevant evidence in their writing to persuade.
- Acknowledge reasons and evidence that are in opposition to their own.
- Use rhetorical appeals in their own writing, including ethos, logos, and pathos, in order to persuade.
- Use rhetorical devices in their own writing in order to persuade.
- Build rhetoric vocabulary.
- Analyze text designed to persuade an audience to do or believe something.
- Identify rhetorical appeals, including ethos, logos, and pathos, in a text.
- Identify rhetorical devices in a text.
- Identify a writer's audience.
- Identify the values and interests of a writer's audience.
- Evaluate the claims made in a text, assessing whether the reasons supporting them are clear and based on relevant evidence.
- Evaluate the credibility of the writer.
- Generate ideas for persuasive speaking and oral advocacy.
- Express ideas clearly and persuasively.
- Use clear reasons and relevant evidence in their speaking to persuade.
- Acknowledge reasons and evidence that are in opposition to their own.
- Identify the values and interests of a speaker's audience.
- Use rhetorical appeals, including ethos, logos, and pathos, in order to persuade.
- Use rhetorical devices in order to persuade.
- Identify rhetorical appeals and devices used by a speaker.
- Analyze rhetorical appeals and devices used by a speaker.
- Use appropriate cadence, volume, and pitch when speaking to an audience in order to persuade.
- Participate as knowledgeable, reflective, and critical members of an engaged citizenry.
- Respond to written and oral presentations using clear reasons and relevant evidence.
- Respond thoughtfully to diverse perspectives.

UNIT 2 OUTLINE

	Big Idea(s)	Overview	Skills
Unit Preassessment			
Lesson 1	≫ Rhetoric is an art that can be systematically studied. ≫ Rhetoricians use a variety of appeals to persuade an audience to do or believe something.	*Welcome to Rhetoric* ≫ Visualization activity. ≫ Journal activity. ≫ Introduction to Aristotle. ≫ Introduction to key terms including rhetoric, logos, ethos, and pathos.	≫ Build rhetoric vocabulary. ≫ Identify rhetorical appeals. ≫ Attend to cadence, volume, and pitch in persuasive speaking.
Lesson 2	≫ Rhetoric is an art that can be systematically studied. ≫ Statements that are true and logical have a natural tendency to prevail over their opposites. ≫ The use of logic and reason, rather than force, to persuade others is a uniquely human capacity. ≫ The ability to evaluate rhetoric used by others is critical to making informed decisions.	*Understanding Rhetoric* ≫ Journal activity. ≫ Introduction to syllogisms and logical fallacies. ≫ Syllogisms and logical fallacies activity. ≫ Introduction to rhetorical devices. ≫ Rhetorical devices activity.	≫ Build rhetoric vocabulary. ≫ Analyze text designed to persuade. ≫ Evaluate claims made in a text. ≫ Identify rhetorical devices in a text.
Formative Assessment 1			
Lesson 3	≫ Rhetoric is an art that can be systematically studied. ≫ Rhetoric serves as a call to action. ≫ Rhetoricians use a variety of appeals to persuade an audience. ≫ Understanding the interests and values of an audience is key to persuasion. ≫ The ability to evaluate rhetoric used by others is critical to making informed decisions.	*Rhetoric in Corporate Advertising* ≫ Journal activity. ≫ The use of appeals in corporate advertising. ≫ View and analyze corporate ads.	≫ Identify values and interests of an audience. ≫ Identify rhetorical appeals and devices used by a speaker. ≫ Analyze rhetorical appeals and devices.
Lesson 4	≫ Rhetoric is an art that can be systematically studied. ≫ Rhetoric is vital to a healthy democracy. ≫ Rhetoric serves as a call to action. ≫ Rhetoricians use a variety of appeals to persuade an audience.	*Rhetoric in Political Advertising* ≫ Journal activity. ≫ Cadence, volume, and pitch analysis. ≫ The use of appeals in political advertising.	≫ Identify values and interests of an audience. ≫ Identify rhetorical appeals and devices used by a speaker. ≫ Analyze rhetorical appeals and devices used by a speaker.

	Big Idea(s)	Overview	Skills
Lesson 4, continued	≫ Understanding the interests and values of an audience is key to persuasion. ≫ Rhetoric can be used to promote or injure the common good. ≫ The ability to evaluate rhetoric used by others is critical to making informed decisions.	≫ View and analyze political ads.	≫ Participate as knowledgeable, reflective, and critical members of an engaged citizenry.
Lesson 5	≫ Rhetoric is an art that can be systematically studied. ≫ Rhetoric is vital to a healthy democracy. ≫ Rhetoric serves as a call to action. ≫ Rhetoricians use a variety of appeals to persuade an audience. ≫ Understanding the interests and values of an audience is key to persuading the audience. ≫ The ability to evaluate rhetoric used by others is critical to making informed decisions.	*Create Your Own Advertisement* ≫ Journal activity. ≫ Cadence, volume, pitch discussion. ≫ Vocal warm-up activity. ≫ Create an original corporate or political advertisement. ≫ Perform corporate or political ads.	≫ Generate ideas for persuasive speaking. ≫ Express ideas clearly and persuasively. ≫ Use clear reasons and relevant evidence. ≫ Identify the values and interests of an audience. ≫ Use rhetorical appeals and devices in their own speaking. ≫ Use appropriate cadence, volume, and pitch when speaking to an audience.
Formative Assessment 2			
Lesson 6	≫ Rhetoric is an art that can be studied systematically. ≫ Rhetoric serves as a call to action. ≫ The use of logic and reason, rather than force, to persuade others is a uniquely human capacity. ≫ Understanding the interests and values of an audience is key to persuasion. ≫ The ability to evaluate rhetoric used by others is critical to making informed decisions. ≫ Rhetoric can be used to promote or injure the common good.	*Epideictic Rhetoric* ≫ Journal activity. ≫ Cadence, volume, and pitch analysis. ≫ Group evaluation of epideictic speech. ≫ Learn to give and receive feedback on oral advocacy.	≫ Participate as knowledgeable, reflective, and critical members of an engaged citizenry. ≫ Build rhetoric vocabulary. ≫ Identify the values and interests of an audience. ≫ Identify and analyze rhetorical appeals and devices.

	Big Idea(s)	Overview	Skills
Lesson 7	≫ Rhetoric is an art that can be studied systematically. ≫ Rhetoric serves as a call to action. ≫ Rhetoric is vital to a healthy democracy. ≫ Rhetoricians use a variety of appeals to persuade an audience. ≫ The use of logic and reason, rather than force, to persuade others to do or believe something is a uniquely human capacity. ≫ Understanding the interests and values of an audience is key to persuasion. ≫ The ability to evaluate rhetoric used by others is critical to making informed decisions. ≫ Statements that are true and logical have a natural tendency to prevail over their opposites.	*Deliberative (Political) Rhetoric* ≫ Journal activity. ≫ Cadence, pitch, and volume analysis. ≫ Group analysis of political (deliberative) speech. ≫ Give and receive feedback on oral advocacy.	≫ Participate as knowledgeable, reflective, creative, and critical members of an engaged citizenry. ≫ Build rhetoric vocabulary. ≫ Identify the values and interests of an audience. ≫ Identify and analyze rhetorical appeals and devices.
Lesson 8	≫ Rhetoric is an art that can be systematically studied. ≫ Rhetoric serves as a call to action. ≫ Rhetoric is vital to a healthy democracy. ≫ Rhetoricians use a variety of appeals to persuade an audience. ≫ The use of logic and reason, rather than force, to persuade others to do or believe something is a uniquely human capacity. ≫ Understanding the interests and values of an audience is key to persuasion. ≫ The ability to evaluate rhetoric used by others is critical to making informed decisions. ≫ Statements that are true and logical have a natural tendency to prevail over their opposites.	*Forensic Rhetoric* ≫ Journal activity. ≫ Cadence, pitch, and volume analysis. ≫ Group analysis of forensic speech. ≫ Give and receive feedback on oral advocacy.	≫ Participate as knowledgeable, reflective, creative, and critical members of an engaged citizenry. ≫ Build rhetoric vocabulary. ≫ Identify the values and interests of an audience. ≫ Identify and analyze rhetorical appeals and devices.

	Big Idea(s)	Overview	Skills
Lesson 9	≫ Rhetoric is an art that can be systematically studied. ≫ Understanding the interests and values of an audience is key to persuasion. ≫ The ability to evaluate rhetoric used by others is critical to making informed decisions. ≫ Statements that are true and logical have a natural tendency to prevail over their opposites.	*Create Your Own Forensic, Epideictic, or Political Speech* ≫ Journal activity. ≫ Vocal warm-up activity. ≫ Cadence, volume, and pitch activity. ≫ Develop an original forensic, epideictic, or deliberative speech using ethos, logos, and/or pathos and additional rhetorical devices.	≫ Participate as knowledgeable, reflective, creative, and critical members of an engaged citizenry. ≫ Build rhetoric vocabulary. ≫ Identify the values and interests of an audience. ≫ Identify and analyze rhetorical appeals and devices. ≫ Generate ideas for persuasive speaking. ≫ Express ideas clearly and persuasively. ≫ Use rhetorical appeals and devices in their own speaking. ≫ Use appropriate cadence, volume, and pitch when speaking to an audience.
Lesson 10	≫ Rhetoric is an art that can be systematically studied. ≫ Understanding the interests and values of an audience is key to persuasion. ≫ The ability to evaluate rhetoric used by others is critical to making informed decisions. ≫ Statements that are true and logical have a natural tendency to prevail over their opposites.	*Perform Your Own Forensic, Epideictic, or Political Speech* ≫ Journal activity. ≫ Vocal warm-up activity. ≫ Cadence, volume, and pitch. ≫ Present an original forensic, epideictic, or deliberative speech using ethos, logos, and/or pathos and additional rhetorical devices.	≫ Participate as knowledgeable, reflective, creative, and critical members of an engaged citizenry. ≫ Identify the values and interests of an audience. ≫ Identify and analyze rhetorical appeals and devices. ≫ Express ideas clearly and persuasively. ≫ Use rhetorical appeals and devices in their own speaking. ≫ Use appropriate cadence, volume, and pitch when speaking to an audience.
Formative Assessment 3			
Lesson 11	≫ Rhetoric is an art that can be systematically studied.	*Research Process Review (Optional)* ≫ Review the research and information seeking strategies from the Exploration and Communication unit. ≫ Begin to think about rhetorical endeavor.	≫ Review and use the research process. ≫ Generate ideas for persuasive speaking and oral advocacy.

	Big Idea(s)	Overview	Skills
Lesson 12	≫ Rhetoric is an art that can be systematically studied. ≫ Understanding the interests and values of an audience is key to persuasion.	*Rhetorical Endeavor Design* ≫ Consider different presentation options. ≫ Begin to design rhetorical endeavors. ≫ Complete rhetorical endeavor design checklist.	≫ Generate ideas for persuasive speaking and oral advocacy. ≫ Participate as knowledgeable, reflective, and critical members of an engaged citizenry.
Lesson 13	≫ Rhetoric is an art that can be systematically studied. ≫ Rhetoricians use a variety of appeals to persuade an audience to do or believe something. ≫ Understanding the interests and values of an audience is key to persuasion.	*Rhetorical Endeavor Research* ≫ Independently conduct research on their rhetorical endeavors.	≫ Participate as knowledgeable, reflective, creative, and critical members of an engaged citizenry. ≫ Generate ideas for persuasive writing and speaking. ≫ Use clear reasons and relevant evidence in persuasive speaking and writing. ≫ Use rhetorical appeals and devices in speaking and writing. ≫ Respond to diverse perspectives.
Lesson 14	≫ Rhetoric is an art that can be systematically studied. ≫ Rhetoricians use a variety of appeals to persuade an audience to do or believe something. ≫ Understanding the interests and values of an audience is key to persuasion.	*Rhetorical Endeavor Writing* ≫ Prepare written portion of rhetorical endeavors.	≫ Participate as knowledgeable, reflective, and critical members of an engaged citizenry. ≫ Use clear reasons and relevant evidence in persuasive speaking and writing. ≫ Use rhetorical appeals and devices in speaking and writing. ≫ Respond to diverse perspectives.
Lesson 15	≫ Rhetoric is an art that can be systematically studied. ≫ Rhetoricians use a variety of appeals to persuade an audience to do or believe something. ≫ Understanding the interests and values of an audience is key to persuasion.	*Practice for Ode to Aristotle Research Gala* ≫ Practice oral portion of rhetorical endeavors. ≫ Practice rhetorical endeavors in front of peers. ≫ Give peer feedback on rhetorical endeavors.	≫ Participate as knowledgeable, reflective, and critical members of an engaged citizenry. ≫ Use clear reasons and relevant evidence in persuasive speaking and writing. ≫ Use rhetorical appeals and devices in speaking and writing.

	Big Idea(s)	Overview	Skills
Lesson 15, continued	≫ The ability to evaluate rhetoric used by others is critical to making informed decisions. ≫ Rhetoricians use a variety of appeals to persuade an audience to do or believe something.		≫ Attend to cadence, volume, and pitch in persuasive speaking. ≫ Respond to diverse perspectives.
Lesson 16	≫ Rhetoric is an art that can be systematically studied. ≫ Rhetoricians use a variety of appeals to persuade an audience to do or believe something. ≫ Understanding the interests and values of an audience is key to persuasion.	*Ode to Aristotle Rhetoric Gala* ≫ Present rhetorical endeavors in front of an audience (summative assessment). ≫ Evaluate the rhetorical endeavor of peers (performance assessment).	≫ Participate as knowledgeable, reflective, and critical members of an engaged citizenry.
Performance Assessment **Summative Assessment**			

PREPARING TO TEACH THE UNIT

RESOURCES AND MATERIALS

Rhetorical exemplars used in the unit are documented in each lesson plan. An important goal for the unit is to help students explore a wide range of topics and examples of rhetoric. Teachers are encouraged to have a collection of speeches, commercials, eulogies, and other rhetorical examples appropriate for a broad range of interests, learning profiles, and reading and comprehension levels available in the classroom. Teachers are also encouraged to share some of their favorite rhetorical examples with students, to invite students to share or bring in rhetorical examples they enjoy, and to explore local opportunities for hearing live persuasive activities (or even invite a practicing lawyer, local politician, or advertiser to visit the classroom).

In order to respond to student diversity, students should be given the opportunity to select rhetorical exemplars that reflect a variety of cultures and backgrounds. Attention should be given to tailoring instructional strategies and activities to address learners with disabilities in the gifted classroom.

Each student will require a composition book for the unit. The composition book will be a workbook, in which students can complete class writing activities, jot down ideas, and work on drafts of their rhetorical endeavors. They should be encouraged to make mistakes in this book, as they should be experimenting with rhetorical devices, words, and ideas. The workbooks will also be used for keeping important handouts and worksheets (such as the excerpts from Aristotle's *Rhetoric*, important unit vocabulary, speeches, etc.). Students will also require a pocket folder, which will include what will become the student's rhetoric journal. In the rhetoric journal, students will write their daily journal entries. These journal entries provide an additional opportunity for teachers to assess student comprehension and progress in the use and evaluation of rhetorical appeals. the rhetoric journal may also be brought home by students to log their personal experiences with persuasion.

Links to web-based lesson materials are available in each lesson plan and on the book's webpage at http://www.routledge.com/assets/clientpages/Research_Rhetoric.aspx.

CLASSROOM ENVIRONMENT

The teacher is encouraged to set up a classroom environment that is conducive to the exploration and enjoyment of rhetoric. For example, the teacher might start a "rhetoric wall," which can be used to display (1) copies of the speeches read or heard in class; (2) examples of rhetorical exemplars recommended by students; (3) information about the lives and work of specific oral advocates, politicians, individuals featured in commercials or eulogies, etc.; (4) journal entries written by students; (5) and interesting ideas from Aristotle's *Rhetoric*. It is also important to have areas of the classroom that work well for individual work, small-group work, and for whole-group discussions and activities (preferably apart from desks) as students will engage in a variety of learning experiences utilizing different grouping arrangements.

CLASSROOM MANAGEMENT

This unit incorporates many different types of activities, from independent work, to creative visualization, to rhetorical demonstration, to group work. Students will sometimes be grouped by readiness levels, sometimes by common interests, and sometimes by preferred ways of learning or working. In other words, there will be much movement and changing from one activity to another. Some students and some groups will manage this type of learning environment better than others. This means that the teacher might need to work with students on how to manage transitions and routines that could be unfamiliar. The teacher might need to explain that because all students are different, there will be times when several different activities are going on at once, or that students will be working from different lists of words. The teacher might also need to explain that there are many different ideas about politics, politicians, and people, but it is important to be respectful of different points of view when analyzing rhetoric. Because of the varied grouping arrangements throughout the unit, it might also be helpful for students to practice moving (and perhaps rearranging the furniture) from small groups, to individual desks, to the space dedicated to group discussion and unit activities prior to the start of the unit.

ONGOING ASSESSMENT

The unit preassessment is administered to students prior to the first lesson. The purposes of the preassessment are (1) to assess what students already know about rhetoric and the means of persuading an audience, which will help tailor the activities and group students appropriately; and (2) to provide a baseline for comparison at the end of the unit so that the teacher can assess the growth of each student throughout the course of the unit.

Ongoing formative assessment, including both formal and informal assessments, are used throughout the unit. Formal formative assessments are administered to students throughout the unit in order to: (1) assess what students already know about rhetoric, which will help tailor the activities and group students appropriately; (2) assess students' developing skills so that resources and activities can be tailored to each student; and (3) provide additional student data throughout the unit for comparison at the end of the unit so that the teacher can assess the growth and progress of each student. Copies of each formal assessment task are included in the resource section after the lesson in which they should be administered. Informal assessments, including journal entries and activities where students create speeches and advertisements, supplement the formal assessments in the unit to provide additional data for student evaluation and progress monitoring.

There are two summative assessments for this unit. The first is the culminating project ending in the Ode to Aristotle Rhetoric Gala in which each student independently creates a rhetorical endeavor to perform in front of an audience. The students' final products will serve as the evidence of their learning and the provided rubric will serve as the evaluation tool. The second is a performance task conducted the day after the rhetoric gala in which students evaluate the rhetorical endeavor of a peer. All of the necessary materials are provided for this assignment.

THE CLEAR CURRICULUM MODEL

This unit has been designed using the CLEAR Curriculum Model. The CLEAR (Challenge Leading to Engagement, Achievement, and Results) Curriculum incorporates elements from three research-based curriculum models: differentiation, Depth and Complexity, and the Schoolwide Enrichment Model by Carol Tomlinson, Sandy Kaplan, and Joseph Renzulli, respectively.

These elements are applied to a curriculum framework that is consistent with state and national standards in reading, but build layers of challenge and opportunities for more in-depth study authentic to the work of professionals within a discipline, to better meet the needs of all students. Refer to page 15 for more information about the CLEAR Curriculum Model.

ICONS EXPLAINED

Integrated throughout the lesson plans are a series of icons or symbols intended to draw your attention to the particular content focus, learning objective, or instructional configuration of each learning activity. Some of these icons are derived from Sandra Kaplan's Depth and Complexity curriculum model, while others have been developed specifically for the CLEAR Curriculum Model used in these units. Refer to page 16 for an explanation of each icon.

LESSON 1 Welcome To Rhetoric

MATERIALS

- ✓ Student journals
- ✓ Student workbooks
- ✓ Handout 1.1: Unit Preassessment
- ✓ Handout 1.2A Excerpts From *Rhetoric* (hardest)
- ✓ Handout 1.2B: Excerpts From *Rhetoric* (on-level)
- ✓ Handout 1.2C: Excerpts From *Rhetoric* (easiest)
- ✓ Handout 1.3: *Rhetoric* Reading Guide
- ✓ Appendix B1: Grouping Plan Chart

- Rhetoric is an art that can be systematically studied.
- Rhetoricians use a variety of appeals to persuade an audience to do or believe something.

OBJECTIVES

Students will:

- ✓ build rhetoric vocabulary, and
- ✓ identify rhetorical appeals, including ethos, logos, and pathos, in a text.

- Rhetoric
- Ethos
- Pathos
- Logos

SEQUENCE

UNIT PREASSESSMENT

1. Administer the Unit Preassessment (Handout 1.1). Explain to students that this assessment is not for a grade. Rather, it is to find out how much they already know about what they are about to learn.
2. **Using the assessment data:** Use students' responses on the preassessment to assess their ability to make predictions about key terms and concepts they will learn in this unit (i.e., ethos, pathos, and logos) and their ability to analyze and understand excerpts from Aristotle's *Rhetoric*, Book II. Sort students into three readiness groups. A sorting chart is provided (Appendix B1):
   - ✓ **Group A:** Students correctly identified words with roots in common with ethos, pathos, and logos; made reasonable predictions about their meaning; and demonstrated the ability to accurately analyze an excerpt from Aristotle's *Rhetoric*.
   - ✓ **Group B:** Students correctly identified words with roots in common with ethos, pathos, and logos or made reasonable predictions about their meaning, and demonstrated some ability to accurately analyze an excerpt from Aristotle's *Rhetoric*.
   - ✓ **Group C:** Students did not demonstrate the ability to identify words with roots in common with ethos, pathos, and logos, or make reasonable predictions about their meaning, and demonstrated no or limited ability to accurately analyze an excerpt from Aristotle's *Rhetoric*.

- Keep in mind that the three readiness groups are suggested or potential groups, but for a given class of students, not all might be applicable. For example, all of your students might fall into Groups B and C, or all might fall into Groups A and B, etc. In that case, in Lesson 1 you may not need to use all three versions of the task.
- Put completed preassessments and *Rhetoric* excerpts (Handouts 1.1–1.2) in student workbooks, as they will be used again in subsequent lessons.

WARM UP

3. Explain to students that they are about to embark on a unit that will help build their oral advocacy skills, and that good oral advocates need to exercise their voices and bodies.

Invite students to stand up, close their eyes, and relax by taking deep breaths from their diaphragm (continue instructing students to breathe deeply until the room is quiet). Engage students in stretching for 2–3 minutes. For example, ask students to reach up to the ceiling as high as they can, and then slowly stretch down to their toes, to stretch from side to side with one arm over their head, to roll their shoulders and head around, etc.

This activity can also be done with students sitting at their desks with eyes closed, but the opportunity to stand up is likely to catch students' attention, facilitate stretching, and help them feel looser.

4. Say: *Now we're going to stretch our tongues and lips and warm up our ability to enunciate with a tongue twister or two. Repeat the words "unique New York" as many times and as quickly as you can without any mispronunciations.* After approximately 20–30 seconds, say: *Let's*

try another one. Repeat the words "black bug's blood" as many times and as quickly as you can without any mispronunciations. Let students work on this tongue twister for approximately 20–30 seconds.

5. Tell students that they will engage in these warm-up activities throughout the unit because strong rhetoricians should always warm up and exercise their voices before trying to convince an audience to do or believe something.
6. Say: *Go back to your desks and think about a time when you tried to persuade someone—a friend, parent, coach, sibling, anyone—to do or believe something. Try to remember as many details as you can about the event that come into your mind. What did you want that person to do or believe? Why? What did you say to persuade him or her? Why did you choose the words you used? Were you successful—did you get the person to do or believe what you wanted? I will give you 30 seconds to quietly get a clear memory of that time with lots of details in your mind.*

- Make sure students have their journals and something to write with already out on their desks or next to them on the floor to make the transition as smooth as possible.
- As they journal, make sure students know that they will have a chance to share their memories/journal entries with the group, but *not yet*. Their job at this stage is to get the details down quickly in their own notebooks in preparation for the next task.

After the 30 seconds are up, ask students to describe (in writing or a drawing) in their journal the time they remembered trying to persuade someone to do or believe something. Let students know that they only have a couple of minutes to get down as many details as they can.

2E

Some 2E students who struggle with the writing process might prefer to bullet short sentences or even draw the images rather than write them.

7. Gather the whole group back together. Give students a chance to share their memories of when they tried to persuade someone to do or believe something.

For some groups, you may need to have students recall what makes a good listener.

Ask: *What did you notice about the responses? Did you notice any common strategies we have used when trying to persuade others?* Students might need some prompting, but they will probably notice that everyone came up with different memories but some similar strategies to persuade. For example, some probably used logic, while others used emotional strategies. This observation is important, since it can lead you to introduce a big idea about rhetoric: People use different strategies in trying to persuade depending on the person or audience they are trying to persuade. This is one secret to being a strong rhetorician—knowing your audience. Let students know that they will be exploring this very important concept known by the best oral advocates as they read, analyze, write, and create great rhetorical examples over the next few weeks.

INSTRUCTION: INTRODUCING VOCABULARY WORDS

8. Write the vocabulary words (*rhetoric*, *ethos*, *logos*, and *pathos*) on the blackboard or whiteboard. Explain that these words will become very

important in their study of rhetoric and the art of persuasion over the next few weeks. Students do not need to write these down. They will be seeing these words again and again throughout the unit and they will read Aristotle's definitions as well.

- Using student responses on the preassessment, determine if it is necessary to review the Greek roots of ethos (moral, showing moral character), pathos (feeling, passion), and logos (to reason, order).
- If students were able to generate words sharing the same roots and predict their meanings, you may briefly discuss some of the words identified by the students that share the same Greek root as ethos (ethics, ethical, etc.), logos (logic, logical, logarithm, etc.), and pathos (sympathy, empathy, psychopath, etc.).
- If some or all students were not able to generate words sharing the same roots and closely predict their meanings, you might do a whole class or small group mini-lesson to help students understand the Greek roots of ethos, pathos, and logos; to identify additional words sharing the same roots; and to predict their possible meanings in the context of understanding persuasion.

INSTRUCTION: ARISTOTLE'S *RHETORIC*

9. In *Rhetoric*, Book I, Aristotle identifies the three means for persuading an audience—ethos, pathos, and logos. Explain to students that they are going to read Aristotle to build their understanding of the meaning of these words. For many students, reading this text will be challenging.

- *Rhetoric* by Aristotle was written in 350 B.C.E. In the translation by W. Rhys Roberts, *Rhetoric* is divided into three books. This translation is available at http://classics.mit.edu/Aristotle/rhetoric.html.
- Historical Context: Aristotle was an Ancient Greek philosopher who lived from approximately 384 B.C.E. to 322 B.C.E. When he was 17, he enrolled in Plato's Academy, the premier learning institution of the day. Together with Socrates and Plato, Aristotle is credited with laying much of the foundation for Western philosophy. Aristotle is also credited with developing the basic system for studying rhetoric, which he defined as the "art of persuasion."

Differentiated excerpts of relevant portions of *Rhetoric* are provided (Handouts 1.2 A–C). According to the preassessment groups, put students into groups and distribute Handouts 1.2 A–C and Handout 1.3.

10. Tell students that, with their group members, they will read the excerpts provided (Handouts 1.2 A–C) and attempt to understand and analyze the meaning of Aristotle's words and the three means of persuasion. Instruct students to use the *Rhetoric* Reading Guide (Handout 1.3) to

structure their reading and to build consensus in the group as to the meaning of the text.

11. You will support groups as they come to consensus on the meaning of Aristotle's definitions of rhetoric, ethos, pathos, and logos. Some groups (students in Group C, for example) might need more support than others in working toward understanding the text.
12. When students have completed their guides, reassemble the class to discuss what they understand the words rhetoric, ethos, logos, and pathos to mean according to Aristotle. It is important that students develop a clear understanding of these terms, as they are foundational to the unit. Write the definitions of the words on the class vocabulary list if one will be used. Alternatively, students should write the definitions of these words in their rhetoric journals.
13. Students should understand that ethos is an appeal to the audience's beliefs or perceptions about the moral character or credibility of the speaker. Students should understand that pathos is an appeal to the audience's emotions. Students should understand that logos is an appeal to what the audience believes is logical; logos typically relies on data, facts, statistics, figures, etc.
14. Students should put the copies of Handouts 1.1 and 1.2 in their student workbooks for future reference. They will be used in subsequent lessons.

CLOSE

15. Ask students to look back at their journal entries. Based on the definitions of ethos, pathos, and logos the students developed, students should identify which appeal they used in the event they described in their journals.
16. Explain to students that each lesson for the next few weeks will begin with a journal entry like the one that opened today's lesson, where their job is to reflect on situations in which they (or others) have used ethos, logos, and/or pathos to persuade someone to do or believe something. Explain that each day during the unit, students will turn to the person next to them and share their rhetorical experiences. Their partner will be asked to identify whether ethos, pathos, or logos was used. Tell students they can use their rhetoric journals to jot down incidents during the day where they use rhetoric in their interactions with friends, teachers, parents, etc.

PREPARATION: FOR NEXT LESSON

17. Read through student journal entries to monitor students' baseline understanding and application of key terms in the unit. If any student appears to be confused, provide clarifying comments for feedback in the journal.

HANDOUT 1.1

UNIT PREASSESSMENT

Directions: Answer the following questions. Use a separate sheet of paper if necessary.

1. What do you think the word *rhetoric* means?

2. Does the word *rhetoric* have a positive or negative connotation? Neither? Explain your answer.

3. When you want to persuade someone to do or believe something, what do you say? What strategy or strategies do you use?

4. What is the most effective strategy someone can use to persuade you to do or believe something?

5. What is the least effective strategy someone can use to persuade you to do or believe something?

HANDOUT 1.1, CONTINUED

6. Three words that you will become familiar with in this unit are *logos, pathos,* and *ethos*. Do they share common roots with other words you know? What are they?

7. Do these words/roots (from your response in Question 6) give you any clues about the meaning of the words *logos, pathos, ethos*? What do you predict is the meaning of these words?

8. Below you will find an excerpt from Book II of Aristotle's *Rhetoric*. Please read this excerpt:

   > There are three things which inspire confidence in the orator's own character—the three, namely, that induce us to believe a thing apart from any proof of it: good sense, good moral character, and goodwill. False statements and bad advice are due to one or more of the following three causes. Men either form a false opinion through want of good sense; or they form a true opinion, but because of their moral badness do not say what they really think; or finally, they are both sensible and upright, but not well disposed to their hearers, and may fail in consequence to recommend what they know to be the best course. These are the only possible cases. It follows that any one who is thought to have all three of these good qualities will inspire trust in his audience. The way to make ourselves thought to be sensible and morally good must be gathered from the analysis of goodness already given: the way to establish your own goodness is the same as the way to establish that of others. Good will and friendliness of disposition will form part of our discussion of the emotions, to which we must now turn.

   In your own words, what do you think this excerpt means?

HANDOUT 1.2A

EXCERPTS FROM *RHETORIC*

EXCERPTS FROM BOOK I, CHAPTER 2

Rhetoric may be defined as the faculty of observing in any given case the available means of persuasion. This is not a function of any other art. Every other art can instruct or persuade about its own particular subject-matter; for instance, medicine about what is healthy and unhealthy, geometry about the properties of magnitudes, arithmetic about numbers, and the same is true of the other arts and sciences. But rhetoric we look upon as the power of observing the means of persuasion on almost any subject presented to us; and that is why we say that, in its technical character, it is not concerned with any special or definite class of subjects . . . .

Of the modes of persuasion furnished by the spoken word there are three kinds. The first kind depends on the personal character of the speaker; the second on putting the audience into a certain frame of mind; the third on the proof, or apparent proof, provided by the words of the speech itself. Persuasion is achieved by the speaker's personal character when the speech is so spoken as to make us think him credible. We believe good men more fully and more readily than others: this is true generally whatever the question is, and absolutely true where exact certainty is impossible and opinions are divided. This kind of persuasion, like the others, should be achieved by what the speaker says, not by what people think of his character before he begins to speak. It is not true, as some writers assume in their treatises on rhetoric, that the personal goodness revealed by the speaker contributes nothing to his power of persuasion; on the contrary, his character may almost be called the most effective means of persuasion he possesses.

Secondly, persuasion may come through the hearers, when the speech stirs their emotions. Our judgements when we are pleased and friendly are not the same as when we are pained and hostile. It is towards producing these effects, as we maintain, that present-day writers on rhetoric direct the whole of their efforts. This subject shall be treated in detail when we come to speak of the emotions.

Thirdly, persuasion is effected through the speech itself when we have proved a truth or an apparent truth by means of the persuasive arguments suitable to the case in question.

There are, then, these three means of effecting persuasion. The man who is to be in command of them must, it is clear, be able (1) to reason logically, (2) to understand human character and goodness in their various forms, and (3) to understand the emotions—that is, to name them and describe them, to know their causes and the way in which they are excited . . . .

HANDOUT 1.2A, CONTINUED

EXCERPTS FROM BOOK III, CHAPTER 1

We have already specified the sources of persuasion. We have shown that these are three in number; what they are; and why there are only these three: for we have shown that persuasion must in every case be effected either (1) by working on the emotions of the [audience members] themselves, (2) by giving them the right impression of the speakers' character, or (3) by proving the truth of the statements made . . . .

Our next subject will be the style of expression. For it is not enough to know what we ought to say; we must also say it as we ought; much help is thus afforded towards producing the right impression of a speech. The first question to receive attention was naturally the one that comes first naturally—how persuasion can be produced from the facts themselves. The second is how to set these facts out in language. A third would be the proper method of delivery; this is a thing that affects the success of a speech greatly; but hitherto the subject has been neglected . . . . It is, essentially, a matter of the right management of the voice to express the various emotions—of speaking loudly, softly, or between the two; of high, low, or intermediate pitch; of the various rhythms that suit various subjects. These are the three things—volume of sound, modulation of pitch, and rhythm—that a speaker bears in mind.

HANDOUT 1.2B

EXCERPTS FROM *RHETORIC*

EXCERPTS FROM BOOK I, CHAPTER 2

Rhetoric may be defined as the faculty of observing in any given case the available means of persuasion. This is not a function of any other art. Every other art can instruct or persuade about its own particular subject-matter; for instance, medicine about what is healthy and unhealthy, geometry about the properties of magnitudes, arithmetic about numbers, and the same is true of the other arts and sciences. But rhetoric we look upon as the power of observing the means of persuasion on almost any subject presented to us; and that is why we say that, in its technical character, it is not concerned with any special or definite class of subjects . . . .

Of the modes of persuasion furnished by the spoken word there are three kinds. The first kind depends on the personal character of the speaker; the second on putting the audience into a certain frame of mind; the third on the proof, or apparent proof, provided by the words of the speech itself. Persuasion is achieved by the **speaker's personal character** when the speech is so spoken as to make us think him credible. We believe good men more fully and more readily than others: this is true generally whatever the question is, and absolutely true where exact certainty is impossible and opinions are divided. This kind of persuasion, like the others, should be achieved by what the speaker says, not by what people think of his character before he begins to speak. It is not true, as some writers assume in their treatises on rhetoric, that the personal goodness revealed by the speaker contributes nothing to his power of persuasion; on the contrary, his character may almost be called the most effective means of persuasion he possesses.

Secondly, persuasion may come through the **hearers**, when **the speech stirs their emotions**. Our judgements when we are pleased and friendly are not the same as when we are pained and hostile. It is towards producing these effects, as we maintain, that present-day writers on rhetoric direct the whole of their efforts. This subject shall be treated in detail when we come to speak of the emotions.

Thirdly, persuasion is effected through **the speech itself** when we have proved a truth or an apparent truth by means of the persuasive arguments suitable to the case in question.

There are, then, these three means of effecting persuasion. The man who is to be in command of them must, it is clear, be able (1) to reason logically, (2) to understand human character and goodness in their various forms, and (3) to understand the emotions—that is, to name them and describe them, to know their causes and the way in which they are excited . . . .

HANDOUT 1.2B, CONTINUED

EXCERPTS FROM BOOK III, CHAPTER 1

We have already specified the **sources of persuasion**. We have shown that these are **three** in number; what they are; and why there are only these three: for **we have shown that persuasion must in every case be effected either (1) by working on the emotions of the [audience members] themselves, (2) by giving them the right impression of the speakers' character, or (3) by proving the truth of the statements made** . . . .

Our next subject will be the style of expression. **For it is not enough to know what we ought to say; we must also say it as we ought**; much help is thus afforded towards producing the right impression of a speech. The first question to receive attention was naturally the one that comes first naturally—how persuasion can be produced from the facts themselves. The second is how to set these facts out in language. A third would be the proper method of **delivery**; this is a thing that affects the success of a speech greatly; but hitherto the subject has been neglected . . . . It is, essentially, a matter of the right management of the voice to express the various emotions—of speaking loudly, softly, or between the two; of high, low, or intermediate pitch; of the various rhythms that suit various subjects. These are the **three things—volume of sound, modulation of pitch, and rhythm—that a speaker bears in mind**.

HANDOUT 1.2C

EXCERPTS FROM *RHETORIC*

EXCERPTS FROM BOOK I, CHAPTER 2

Rhetoric may be defined as the faculty of observing in any given case the available means of persuasion. This is not a function of any other art. Every other art can instruct or persuade about its own particular subject-matter; for instance, medicine about what is healthy and unhealthy, geometry about the properties of magnitudes, arithmetic about numbers, and the same is true of the other arts and sciences. But rhetoric we look upon as the power of observing the means of persuasion on almost any subject presented to us . . . .

Of the modes of persuasion furnished by the spoken word there are three kinds. The first kind depends on the **personal character of the speaker**; the second on putting the audience into a certain frame of mind; the third on the proof, or apparent proof, provided by the words of the speech itself. Persuasion is achieved by the **speaker's personal character** when the speech is so spoken as to make us think him credible . . . .

Secondly, persuasion may come through the **hearers**, when **the speech stirs their emotions.** Our judgements when we are pleased and friendly are not the same as when we are pained and hostile . . . .

Thirdly, persuasion is effected through **the speech itself** when we have **proved a truth** or an apparent truth by means of the persuasive arguments suitable to the case in question.

There are, then, these three means of effecting persuasion. The man who is to be in command of them must, it is clear, be able (1) to reason logically, (2) to understand human character and goodness in their various forms, and (3) to understand the emotions—that is, to name them and describe them, to know their causes and the way in which they are excited . . . .

EXCERPTS FROM BOOK III, CHAPTER 1

We have already specified the **sources of persuasion.** We have shown that these are **three** in number; what they are; and why there are only these three: for **we have shown that persuasion must in every case be effected either (1) by working on the emotions of the [audience members] themselves [pathos], (2) by giving them the right impression of the speakers' character [ethos], or (3) by proving the truth of the statements made [logos]** . . . .

Our next subject will be the style of expression. **For it is not enough to know what we ought to say; we must also say it as we ought**; much help is thus afforded towards producing the right impression of a speech . . . . [An orator must pay attention to] the proper method of **delivery** . . . . It is, essentially, a matter of the right management of the voice to express the various emo-

HANDOUT 1.2C, CONTINUED

tions—of speaking loudly, softly, or between the two; of high, low, or intermediate pitch; of the various rhythms that suit various subjects. These are the **three things—volume of sound, modulation of pitch, and rhythm—that a speaker bears in mind.**

HANDOUT 1.3

RHETORIC READING GUIDE

Directions: This reading guide is designed to assist you and your group in understanding Aristotle's *Rhetoric*. Use a separate sheet of paper if necessary.

1. Read the excerpts from Book I, Chapter 2 of Aristotle's *Rhetoric*. In your own words, define the word *rhetoric*. Why does Aristotle refer to rhetoric as an "art"?

2. Aristotle articulates three modes of persuasion in *Rhetoric* including ethos, pathos, and logos. These three modes of persuasion are often called "appeals." In your own words, summarize the three modes of persuasion. Use your understanding of the Greek roots of ethos, pathos, and logos to help you understand what these appeals mean and how they can be used to persuade.
   a. First mode of persuasion.

   Does this mean of persuasion refer to ethos, pathos, or logos? ____________________

   b. Second mode of persuasion.

   Does this mean of persuasion refer to ethos, pathos, or logos? ____________________

HANDOUT 1.3, CONTINUED

c. Third mode of persuasion.

Does this mean of persuasion refer to ethos, pathos, or logos? ______________

3. Read the excerpts from Book III, Chapter 1 of Aristotle's *Rhetoric.* Aristotle says that good oral advocates pay attention to both what is said and how it is said, or its style. He urges speakers to use proper "sound" (or volume), "pitch" and "rhythm" (or cadence) when speaking in order to be more persuasive. Do you agree with Aristotle? Why or why not?

LESSON 2 Understanding Rhetoric

MATERIALS

- ✓ Student journals
- ✓ Student workbooks
- ✓ Handout 2.1: Syllogisms and Logical Fallacies
- ✓ Handout 2.2: Rhetoric Terminology: Rhetorical Devices

- Rhetoric is an art that can be systematically studied.
- Statements that are true and logical have a natural tendency to prevail over their opposites.
- The use of logic and reason, rather than force, to persuade others is a uniquely human capacity.
- The ability to evaluate rhetoric used by others is critical to making informed decisions.

OBJECTIVES

Students will:

- ✓ build rhetoric vocabulary,
- ✓ identify and analyze rhetorical text designed to persuade, and
- ✓ evaluate claims made in a text.

- Logos
- Syllogism
- Logical fallacy

SEQUENCE

WARM UP

1. Hold a short question-and-answer session asking students to review the definitions/concepts they examined yesterday, including rhetoric, ethos, logos, and pathos.
2. Use the question-and-answer review, along with the journal exercise, to monitor student progress and baseline understanding of the definition of rhetoric and rhetorical appeals.
3. Say: *We're going to get started on our daily rhetoric journal reflection. First let me share an example of a time I tried to persuade someone and which rhetorical appeal I used (see Tip Box). Now it's your turn. Close your eyes and think about another time when you tried to persuade someone—a time different than you thought of yesterday—to do or believe something. Try to remember as many details as you can about the event that comes into your mind. What did you want that person to do or believe? Why? What did you say to persuade him or her? Why did you choose the words you used? Did you use ethos, pathos, or logos? Were you successful—did you get the person to do or believe what you wanted? I will give you 30 seconds to quietly get a clear memory of that time with lots of details in your mind.*

Think Aloud Strategy: Model a metacognitive dialogue with yourself that reflects your thought process concerning a time you tried to persuade someone to do or believe something. Provide rich details to your students, identify which of Aristotle's appeals you used to persuade, and reflect on whether or not you were successful.

4. After the 30 seconds are up, ask students to describe (in writing or a drawing) in their journal the time they remembered trying to persuade someone to do or believe something. Remind students that they only have a couple of minutes to get down as many details as they can.

2E

Remember, if you have students who struggle with written expression, they may draw this memory or bullet point in short phrases with as many details as possible.

5. Ask students to turn to their neighbor and share their memories. Ask partners to identify the rhetorical appeal used by their partners.
6. To ensure that students are on track at this point in the unit, ask students to share with the whole class their rhetorical memories and what rhetorical appeal was used. Use this discussion to clarify any baseline misunderstanding students may have about ethos, logos, and pathos.

ACTIVITY: SYLLOGISMS

Pair students by readiness as indicated on the preassessment. Tell partners to pick one of their desks, or another comfortable place in the classroom to work from.

7. Explain to students that they will continue to build their rhetoric vocabulary and understanding of logical arguments. Distribute Handout 2.1.

You might prefer small groups of 3–4 students based on readiness rather than pairs.

Tell students that Aristotle explained in the *Rhetoric* that syllogisms can be used as a tool for understanding arguments using logical and deductive reasoning. Also explain that understanding syllogisms can both help students create more persuasive arguments and detect arguments that are not based on logic.

8. Read the first example of the logical syllogism on Handout 2.1. Explain the concepts of major and minor premises, and the necessary conclusion of logical, or valid, arguments. Ask students to independently create a logical syllogism like the one created by Aristotle. Students may need notepaper for this.
9. Ask two or three students to share their syllogisms with the class. Make sure that they are valid and logical. If they are not, brainstorm with the class how to change the syllogism to make it valid and logical.
10. Next, instruct students to work through the syllogisms worksheet in their pairs or small groups. You should circulate through the classroom to check for understanding. You may need to provide support to some students during this activity, particularly those who demonstrated less understanding in the preassessment.
11. Once all students have completed the syllogisms worksheet, review the answers as a class. Again, check for understanding and clarify any misunderstandings that are evident from the classroom discussion. Tell students to put their syllogisms and rhetorical devices handouts in their workbooks for future reference.

ACTIVITY: RHETORICAL DEVICES

12. Distribute Handout 2.2: Rhetoric Terminology: Rhetorical Devices. Explain to students that over the next several lessons they will be examining examples of rhetoric in advertising and famous speeches. Explain that they will analyze how great orators use rhetorical appeals, and also

Students will begin to look for the use of rhetorical devices in the next several lessons when the class analyzes advertising and great speeches. These rhetorical devices are typically used to emphasize and highlight certain points that the speaker/writer believes makes a speech or text more persuasive. For today, you are simply identifying and briefly discussing some additional linguistic tools that can be employed to enhance the persuasiveness of rhetoric.

how they use additional rhetorical devices to more effectively persuade an audience to do or believe something.

Briefly review each of the terms on the Handout 2.2. Ask students if they can think of their own examples of any of the terms. Ask students to predict why these devices might make a speaker or a text more persuasive.

13. Tell students that they will look for these rhetorical devices in the examples of rhetoric they will study over the next several days. Ask students to keep Handout 2.2 in their workbook for later reference.

HOMEWORK

14. Instruct students to find someone outside their classroom—parents, coaches, grandparents, friends, etc.—who can provide an example of how he or she was able to persuade another person to do or believe something. Ask students to decide whether this person used ethos, pathos, or logos and to reflect on why this appeal was effective. Ask students to jot down this example in their Student Journal.

PREPARATION: FOR NEXT LESSON

15. Take a few minutes to review journal responses to check for developing understanding of rhetorical appeals. If students show any misconceptions of rhetorical appeals, provide written feedback to students to clarify misunderstandings.

HANDOUT 2.1

SYLLOGISMS AND LOGICAL FALLACIES

Directions: Syllogisms are a type of logical argument that applies deductive reasoning to arrive at a conclusion. Syllogisms consist of a major premise, a minor premise, and the conclusion. To be a valid—or logical—syllogism, the conclusion must be proven by the major and minor premises. For example:

All men are mortal. (Major premise)
Socrates is a man. (Minor premise)
Socrates is mortal. (Conclusion)

Everyone in this class is tired. (Major premise)
I'm in this class. (Minor premise)
I am tired. (Conclusion)

Arguments may be valid or logical even if they are untrue:
All dogs can fly.
Fido is a dog.
Fido can fly.

Carefully study the following syllogisms and decide if they are valid or invalid.

1. All zebras are striped animals.
   No zebras are polar bears.
   Therefore, no polar bears are striped animals.

   ❑ Valid ❑ Invalid

2. All clowns are funny individuals.
   Some sad people are clowns.
   Therefore, some sad people are funny individuals.

   ❑ Valid ❑ Invalid

3. Some sticky substances are yucky things.
   All taffy is a sticky substance.
   Therefore, some taffy is a yucky thing.

   ❑ Valid ❑ Invalid

HANDOUT 2.1, CONTINUED

4. All items made of gold are expensive items.
   Some rings are items made of gold.
   Therefore, some rings are expensive items.

   ❑ Valid ❑ Invalid

5. All flies are winged creatures.
   All butterflies are winged creatures.
   Therefore, all butterflies are flies.

   ❑ Valid ❑ Invalid

Directions: The following are examples of syllogisms that are missing the conclusions. Study the two reasons very carefully and complete the syllogism with the conclusion that logically follows.

1. All fragile things are breakable things.
   Some glasses are fragile things.
   Therefore, ______________________________.

2. All mammals are warm-blooded animals.
   All whales are mammals.
   Therefore, ______________________________.

3. All books are things with pages.
   Some books are mysteries.
   Therefore, ______________________________.

Directions: Create two valid syllogisms.

1. ______________________________

   ____

   ____

2. ______________________________

   ____

   ____

HANDOUT 2.1, CONTINUED

Directions: Create two invalid syllogisms.

1. ______________________________

____

____

2. ______________________________

____

____

Directions: Create your own example of a syllogism that is missing a conclusion or a minor premise. Share your example with a partner and see if they can solve it.

HANDOUT 2.2

RHETORIC TERMINOLOGY: RHETORICAL DEVICES

1. **Ad hominem** arguments attack the credibility of the speaker's opponent rather than using logic. For example, in her acceptance speech at the 2008 Republican National Convention, Sarah Palin says: "I guess a small-town mayor is sort of like a community organizer, except that you have actual responsibilities." Another example is when Draco Malfoy says Hermione Granger can't be an excellent witch because she is a muggle-born.
2. **Alliteration** is the repetition of consonant sounds at the beginning of words. For example, in his 1960 Presidential Inaugural Address, John F. Kennedy stated: "With a good conscience our only sure reward, with history the final judge of our deeds, let us go forth to lead the land we love."
3. **Anaphora** is the repetition of a word or phrase at the *beginning* of successive phrases, clauses or lines. For example, in his second Presidential Inaugural Address in 1865, Abraham Lincoln stated: "With malice toward none; with charity for all; with firmness in the right . . . . "
4. **Antithesis** is the opposition or juxtaposition of ideas or words in a balanced or parallel construction. For example, in his "I Have a Dream" speech, Martin Luther King Jr. says "I have a dream that my four little children will one day live in a nation where they will be judged not by the color of their skin but by the content of their character." Another example is seen in William Shakespeare's *Julius Caesar* when Brutus states: "Not that I loved Caesar less, but that I loved Rome more."
5. **Conduplicatio** or **parallelism** is the repetition of a key word or words *within* or *at the end* of successive phrases or clauses. For example, following Martin Luther King Jr.'s assassination in 1968, Robert F. Kennedy stated: "We will have difficult times. We've had difficult times in the past. And we will have difficult times in the future."
6. **Euphemism** is a substitution of a more pleasant expression for one whose meaning may come across as sad, rude, or offensive. For example, after being diagnosed with a deadly disease in 1939, Lou Gehrig stated: "Fans, for the past two weeks you have been reading about the bad break I got."
7. **Hyperbole** is when a speaker exaggerates for emphasis. For example, after being diagnosed with a deadly disease in 1939, Lou Gehrig stated: "When the New York Giants, a team you would give your right arm to beat, and vice versa, sends you a gift—that's something."
8. **Metaphor** is used to convey to the audience a new idea by comparing two unlike things to each other based on a characteristic in common between them. For example, in her eulogy of Coretta Scott King in 2006, Maya Angelou stated: "In times of interior violent storms she sat, her hands resting in her lap calmly, like good children sleeping."
9. **Paralipsis** is used when a speaker pretends to omit something by drawing attention to it. For example, in a 1984 Presidential debate, Ronald Reagan stated the following about his opponent Walter Mondale: "I will not make age an issue of this campaign. I am not going to exploit, for political purposes, my opponent's youth and inexperience."

LESSON

3 Rhetoric in Corporate Advertising

MATERIALS

- ✓ Student journals
- ✓ Student workbooks
- ✓ Corporate advertising videos (available on YouTube):
  - "The North Face: This Land" (available at https://www.youtube.com/watch?v=tll-4WONtg0)
  - "Nike Soccer: The Last Game" (available at https://www.youtube.com/watch?v=afUUBvWBp3I)
  - "Sarah McLachlan SPCA Commercial" (available at https://www.youtube.com/watch?v=IO9d2PpP7tQ)
  - "Meet BP's Janet Weiss, President of BP Alaska" (for formative assessment, available at https://www.youtube.com/watch?v=CJYZZRY11z0)
- ✓ Handout 3.1: Rhetorical Appeal and Device Identifier (four copies per student)

- Rhetoric is an art that can be systematically studied.
- Rhetoric serves as a call to action.
- Rhetoricians use a variety of appeals to persuade an audience.
- Understanding the interests and values of an audience is key to persuasion.
- The ability to evaluate rhetoric used by others is critical to making informed decisions.

OBJECTIVES

Students will:

- ✓ build rhetoric vocabulary,
- ✓ identify rhetorical appeals and devices used by a speaker,
- ✓ analyze rhetorical appeals and devices used by a speaker, and
- ✓ identify values and interests of an audience.

- Rhetoric
- Ethos
- Pathos
- Logos

SEQUENCE

You can consider this alternative journaling activity throughout the unit.

- As an introductory activity, all students might wish to identify and describe their personal favorite advertisements. You can take this as an opportunity to come to a class consensus on whether the creator of the advertisement relies on ethos, pathos, and/or logos as a selling point.
- The YouTube videos selected for this lesson exemplify the different ways rhetorical appeals are used in corporate advertising. You might select different ads based on the interests of your students. However, you should select advertisements that also clearly use identifiable rhetorical appeals.

WARM UP

1. Say: *We're going to get started on our daily rhetoric journal reflection. Close your eyes and think about a time when somebody—a friend, parent, coach, sibling, anyone—tried to persuade YOU to do or believe something. Try to remember as many details as you can about the event that comes into your mind. What did that person want you to do or believe? Why? What did that person say to persuade you? Why do you think he or she chose the words he or she used? Did that person use ethos, pathos, or logos? Was that person successful—did he or she get you to do or believe what was wanted? I will give you 30 seconds to quietly get a clear memory of that time with lots of details in your mind.*
2. After the 30 seconds are up, ask students to describe (in writing or a drawing) in their journal the time they remembered someone trying to make them to do or believe something. Remind students that they only have a couple of minutes to get down as many details as they can.
3. Ask students to turn to their neighbor and share their memories. Ask partners to identify the rhetorical appeal used by their partners.

INSTRUCTION: RHETORICAL APPEALS IN ADVERTISING

- Based on your review of student journal responses, it might be necessary to spend a few minutes reviewing rhetorical appeals. It is important that students are able to identify rhetorical appeals in persuasive writing and oratory as they will be responsible for including examples of them in their summative performance assessment. If only a small number of students need to review rhetorical appeals, work with them in a small group.
- For those students who do not need a review, form small groups (3–4 students) and have them discuss some of their favorite commercials and advertisements, noting what they like most about the commercials and if they think there is evidence of ethos, pathos, or logos in them.

4. Distribute Handout 3.1 (three copies per student, a fourth copy will be used for this lesson's formative assessment). Explain to students that they will be viewing several advertisements today, and that the advertisements will contain strong rhetorical appeals. As a whole class, ask the students what they believe the purpose of an advertisement is.

Students should ultimately conclude that a key purpose of corporate advertisements is to get the audience to buy or spend money on something. Explain to students that they will use Handout 3.1 to write their reflections and observations about the rhetorical appeals used by the creators of the advertisements.

- Brainstorm how advertisers can use rhetorical appeals. Tell students that commercials typically have a particular audience in mind, and that what might persuade one audience won't persuade another. Ask students to give examples of a particular commercial that would work for one audience but not another. Ask students why it is important to know your audience when creating advertisements.
- Reinforce this concept by having students consider how advertisers market different audiences in different ways. For example, how might a product be advertised in a hot climate versus a cold one? A rural environment or urban environment? Or, how are some products aimed at younger audiences? This discussion will prepare students for the activities to follow.

Tell students that while they are watching the corporate advertisements selected for this lesson, they should be thinking about what rhetorical appeals are being used, who the audience is likely to be, and whether they think the advertisement has been effective (and for whom).

5. Ask students if they are familiar with The North Face. If not, explain that The North Face makes outdoor and athletic apparel and gear. Ask students to watch and listen carefully to The North Face ad. Ask students to think about what the creator of the ad is trying to get them to do or believe and to watch for the use of rhetorical appeals. After watching, pose the following questions:
   - ✓ What is North Face trying to make you believe or do? How did The North Face try to accomplish this?
   - ✓ Do you recognize the song in the ad ("This Land is Your Land")? Why do you think the creator of the ad chose this song?
   - ✓ Did it use pathos, logos, or ethos in the ad? Where? How? Who is the audience?
   - ✓ What do you think of this commercial? Does it make you want to buy North Face products? Why or why not? Does the creator of the ad ever explicitly say "Buy North Face clothes and gear"? Does this matter?

- Ask students if this advertisement would be effective in their community. Ask them to consider how it might be changed if it were shown in their community.
- Following this discussion, work together with the students to complete Handout 3.1, specifically the sections addressing rhetorical appeals. Check for understanding with a brief follow-up conversation of student responses.

For this lesson, students will not look for rhetorical devices. You should briefly explain that you will focus on the use of ethos, pathos, and logos for today's lesson, and in future lessons students will start to look for additional rhetorical devices.

During the class discussion, you should ensure that students identify the rhetorical appeals. For example, the song in the commercial employs pathos by creating a sense of patriotism in the audience. Patriotism is also appealed to through the use of many images of iconic American scenes and images. Similarly, the smiling, happy, and adventurous people in the commercial reflect the use of pathos as these images are intended to make the audience want to be adventurous and happy as well. Ethos is employed through the great athletes and is designed to make the audience believe they too can be great athletes if they wear The North Face products.

You should be prepared to discuss the use of ethos in this advertisement. Explain that creators of ads often use famous people as an appeal to ethos. In this ad, Nike uses the animated images of world-class soccer players with the purpose of making kids want Nike products, to inspire them to persevere in the face of adversity, and that wearing Nike will help them persevere. Animation is also more appealing to younger viewers who are more likely to be involved in sports. Like The North Face ad, the creators of the Nike ad never explicitly request the viewer to buy Nike products.

6. Ask students to watch and listen carefully to the Nike ad. Ask students to think about what the creator of the ad is trying to get them to do or believe and to watch for the use of rhetorical appeals. After watching, pose the following questions:
   - ✓ What is Nike trying to make you believe or do? How did Nike try to accomplish this?
   - ✓ Why do you think the creator of the advertisement used animation in this ad? Was it effective?
   - ✓ Was pathos, logos, or ethos used in the ad? Where? How? Who is the audience? Adults? Kids? Both?
   - ✓ What do you think of this commercial? Does it make you want to buy Nike products? Why or why not?
   - ✓ Does the creator of the advertisement ever explicitly say "Buy Nike cleats, shirts, and products"? Does this matter?

Following this discussion, have students work in pairs/small groups to complete Handout 3.1, focusing specifically on the sections addressing rhetorical appeals. As students discuss their answers, walk through the classroom to monitor their comprehension. Check for overall class understanding with a brief follow-up conversation that reviews answers on the worksheets.

This is an advertisement created by the Society for the Prevention of Cruelty to Animals (SPCA). It was very successful in raising money for the nonprofit organization. You should use your judgment about showing this advertisement. You should allow those students who do not feel comfortable to be excused from watching. It was selected for its strong use of ethos (Sarah McLaughlin as expert), pathos (the images of animals and the mournful music appeals deeply to emotion), AND logos (data and statistics provided throughout).

7. Ask students to watch and listen carefully to the SPCA ad. Explain to the students that the images may be distressing, but that this commercial is an excellent example of persuasion in advertising. Ask students to think about what the SPCA is trying to get them to do or believe. After watching, pose the following questions:
   - ✓ What is the SPCA trying to make you believe or do? How did the SPCA try to accomplish this?
   - ✓ Why do you think the creator of the advertisement used images of real animals in this ad? Do you agree with this choice?
   - ✓ Did the creator use pathos, logos, or ethos in the ad? Where? How? What was the impact on you?
   - ✓ What do you think of this commercial? Does it make you want to contribute money to the SPCA? Why or why not?

- Following this discussion, ask students to work in pairs/small groups to complete Handout 3.1, focusing specifically on the rhetorical appeals sections. As students discuss their answers, walk through the classroom to monitor their comprehension. Check for overall class understanding with a brief follow-up conversation that reviews answers on the worksheets.
- Ask students to place their completed Handout 3.1 copies in their workbooks. Let students know that they should keep copies of these handouts, as they will refer back to them in later lessons.

PREPARATION: FORMATIVE ASSESSMENT 1

8. Before Lesson 4, administer Formative Assessment 1, using Handout 3.1. Students will view the BP ad and answer the questions on the handout independently.
   - ✓ Before watching, explain that BP released this advertisement after a BP Oil Rig Platform in the Gulf of Mexico exploded. This explosion caused the death of 11 workers, and is considered to be the worst environmental disaster in U.S. history. In addition to the loss of human life, millions of barrels of oil were leaked into the Gulf of Mexico, causing significant pollution to wildlife and natural resources in five states along the Gulf of Mexico.
   - ✓ Explain the circumstances surrounding the BP explosion to the degree you feel is appropriate. This accident caused many people in the U.S. to have negative feelings towards BP, it resulted in the assessment of billions of dollars in fines and legal liability to BP, and it threatened BP's financial success in the United States.
   - ✓ Play the ad. After watching, ask students to think about what BP is trying to get them to do or believe and how the BP tried to accomplish this. Ask students to complete Handout 3.1.

HOMEWORK

9. Tell students that they will continue their examination of rhetoric in advertising during the next lesson. Explain that the focus of the next lesson is political advertisements rather than corporate advertisements. For homework, ask students to speak to a parent, guardian, or other adult about a political advertisement the adult recalls. Students should speak to the adult about why he or she was persuaded and then try to categorize the persuasive technique as ethos, pathos, or logos.

PREPARATION: FOR NEXT LESSON

10. Read student responses to the formative assessment and make notes about students' developing understandings at this point in the unit. As an additional assessment of student progress, review and provide feedback on students' responses on Handout 3.1. If necessary, meet with students who are struggling with unit ideas and skills to clarify misunderstandings.

HANDOUT 3.1

RHETORICAL APPEAL AND DEVICE IDENTIFIER

Rhetorical Exemplar (Commercial, Speech): ______________________

1. What is the author/creator trying to get you to do or believe?

2. What rhetorical appeal(s) is/are being used?

3. Did it/they work? Why or why not?

4. What other rhetorical devices were used?

5. Would you do anything differently to be more persuasive? What?

LESSON

4 Rhetoric in Political Advertising

MATERIALS

- Student journals
- Student workbooks
- Political advertising videos (available on YouTube):
    - John F. Kennedy, 1960: "Kennedy For Me" (available at https://www.youtube.com/watch?v=S6GS4bSvGBg)
    - Lyndon Johnson, 1964: "Daisy Girl" (available at https://www.youtube.com/watch?v=9Id_r6pNsus)
    - Ronald Reagan, 1984: "Morning Again in America" (available at https://www.youtube.com/watch?v=EU-IBF8nwSY)
    - Hillary Clinton, 2008: "3 a.m. at the White House" (available at https://www.youtube.com/watch?v=7yr7odFUARg)

- Handout 3.1: Rhetorical Appeal and Device Identifier (four copies per student)

- Rhetoric is an art that can be systematically studied.
- Rhetoricians use a variety of appeals to persuade an audience.
- Rhetoric is vital to a healthy democracy.
- Understanding the interests and values of an audience is key to persuasion.
- Rhetoric can be used to promote or injure the common good.
- The ability to evaluate the rhetoric used by others is critical to making informed decisions.

OBJECTIVES

Students will:

- identify rhetorical appeals and devices used by a speaker,
- analyze rhetorical appeals and devices used by a speaker, and
- identify values and interests of an audience.

- Ethos
- Pathos
- Logos
- Cadence
- Volume
- Pitch

SEQUENCE

WARM UP

1. Say: *We're going to get started on our daily rhetoric journal reflection. Close your eyes and think about a time when you were persuaded to buy a product after seeing an advertisement about the product. Try to remember as many details as you can about the advertisement that comes into your mind. What did the advertiser want you to believe if you bought its product? What did the advertiser say or show to persuade you? Why did it choose the words used in the advertisement? Did the advertiser use ethos, pathos, or logos? I will give you 30 seconds to quietly get a clear memory of that time with lots of details in your mind.*

Teachers should feel free to tailor the warm-up activity questions as they deem appropriate.

After the 30 seconds are up, ask students to describe (in writing or a drawing) in their journal the time they remembered being persuaded to buy a product after seeing an advertisement about the product. Remind students that they only have a couple of minutes to get down as many details as they can.

2. Ask students to turn to their neighbor and share their memories. Ask partners to identify the rhetorical appeal used in the advertisement shared by their partners.

To monitor comprehension of the use of rhetorical appeals, ask a few students to share their memories about the time he or she was persuaded to buy a product after seeing an advertisement. Ask other students in the classroom to identify the appeal used by the advertiser.

INSTRUCTION: RHETORICAL APPEALS IN POLITICAL ADVERTISING

- Based on student responses to Formative Assessment 1 and student discussion following their journaling activity, it might be necessary to spend a few minutes reviewing rhetorical appeals. It is essential at this point in the unit that students are able to identify rhetorical appeals in persuasive writing and speaking. Students will be responsible for including examples of rhetorical appeals in their summative performance assessment, or rhetorical endeavors to be presented at the Ode to Aristotle Rhetoric Gala.
- If only a small number of students need to review rhetorical appeals, work with them in a small group. For those students who do not need a review, form small groups (3–4 students). Instruct the small groups to discuss some of their favorite political advertisements. Ask groups to discuss what they like most about the advertisements and whether the candidate is using ethos, pathos, and/or logos. If they are not familiar with any political ads, ask them to brainstorm what they would put in an ad if they were running for a school office or leadership position.

The YouTube clips selected for this lesson were chosen as they exemplify the use of rhetorical appeals in political advertising. You might select different ads based on the interests of your students or political candidates from your state/district, but you should select political advertisements that clearly use identifiable rhetorical appeals and devices.

3. **After you have finished the rhetorical devices review (if necessary), distribute copies of Handout 3.1 (four copies each). Ask students to take out Handout 2.2 from their workbooks. Explain to students that they will be viewing political advertisements today.**

Ask the students what they believe the purposes of political advertisements are. Ask students if they have ever seen a political advertisement and what they noticed about it. Students should ultimately conclude that the purpose is to get people to vote for, or believe something about, a political candidate.

Ask students if they can recall a local election, and what they remember about it. Did they see any political advertisements during the election? What were the issues that were important to their community in the election? Ask students: *If you had to make a guess, would you say your community is "conservative" (Republican leaning) or "liberal" (Democrat leaning) and how would that change the political advertisements you might see?*

Brainstorm the possible use of rhetorical appeals in political advertising. Tell students that they will begin to examine not only the use of ethos, pathos, and logos in political advertisements, but also the use of rhetorical devices. Tell students that together the whole class will complete Handout 3.1 after watching the first political advertisement.

Explain to students that the political advertisements they are about to view are regarded as some of the best examples of political advertising in our history.

4. Ask students what they know about John F. Kennedy. Spend as much time as you believe is necessary introducing Kennedy if students are unfamiliar with his presidency. Play the "Kennedy For Me" ad. After watching, pose the following questions:
   - What are your general impressions of this political advertisement? What did you like/not like?
   - Did you notice ethos (pictures of a handsome and smiling Kennedy), pathos (cheerful tune, crowds cheering him, different ages, races, gender), and/or logos?
   - What did the creators of the ad want the audience to do for or believe about Kennedy (vote for him; believe he was qualified and mature enough to be President)?
   - Who do you think the audience was (voting American public, skeptics of his candidacy)?
   - Did you notice the use of any rhetorical devices (e.g., rhetorical questions ["do you think . . . "], repetition ["it's up to you"])? Why do you think the creators of this ad used these devices to convince the audience Kennedy was the best candidate for President? Do you think they were effective?
   - Could you imagine this advertisement being used today? Why or why not?

Some students may not be familiar with the presidency of John Kennedy. Explain to students that many people were concerned that Kennedy was too young to be president, and they were also concerned that he was Catholic. You may need to brief students on Kennedy's opponent (Nixon) and some of Kennedy's strengths (e.g., great communicator, handsome) to contextualize the advertisement.

Be sure to discuss the voice of the speaker in the "Daisy Girl" advertisement. The voice is high pitched, shrill, urgent, and even frightening. The volume is also high. These observations are important, as students will soon start to examine and discuss cadence, volume, and pitch.

5. As a class, complete Handout 3.1 for the Kennedy ad.
6. Ask students what they know about Lyndon Johnson. You may have to spend a little time introducing Johnson if students are unfamiliar with his presidency. Tell students that the ad they are about to watch was shown in September 1964 during his presidential campaign. Play the "Daisy Girl" ad. After watching, pose the following questions:
   - What are your general impressions of this political advertisement? What did you like/not like?

- ✓ Did you notice ethos (the voice of Johnson), pathos (the adorable little girl that could be anyone's child, the ominous countdown, the nuclear explosion), and/or logos (there's not much logos in this ad)?
- ✓ What did the creator of the ad want the audience to do or believe about Johnson (if he's not reelected, we'll go to war and die)?
- ✓ Who do you think the audience was (voting American public)?
- ✓ Did you notice the use of any rhetorical devices (e.g., anaphora ["We must either love each other, or we must die"], euphemism ["These are the stakes—to make a world in which all of God's children can live, or go into the dark"], etc.)? Why do you think Johnson used these devices? Do you think they were effective?
- ✓ What did you notice about the voice of the speaker in the commercial (shrill, anxious)? What do you believe was the intended effect of the voice? How does this advertisement compare to Kennedy's advertisement?

Some students may not be familiar with the presidency of Lyndon Johnson. You may need to brief students on Johnson's opponent (Goldwater) and some of the crises facing Johnson (America's increasing involvement in the Vietnam War, the Cold War, and fears about nuclear war with communist countries, etc.) to contextualize the advertisement. Tell the students that this ad played only once during a football game before it was pulled off the air, but news reports continued to play it as it became controversial.

7. Tell students that the "Daisy Girl" ad was shown on television only once during the Presidential election of 1964. Johnson was criticized for the advertisement. Ask students why they think the advertisement was only shown once and why Johnson was criticized. After discussing the Daisy Girl advertisement, ask students to work with a partner to complete Handout 3.1. As students complete the worksheet, monitor their progress by listening to their conversations and provide appropriate verbal feedback.
8. Ask students what they know about Ronald Reagan. You may have to spend a little time introducing Reagan if students are unfamiliar with his presidency. Tell students Reagan used the political advertisement they are about to watch in his 1984 reelection bid. Play the "Morning Again in America" ad. After watching the advertisement, pose the following questions:
   - ✓ What are your general impressions of this political advertisement? What did you like/not like?
   - ✓ Did you notice ethos (Reagan himself), pathos (the music, the happy images, the flag, etc.), and/or logos (statistics about inflation, jobs, etc.)?

- ✓ What did the creator of the ad want the audience to do or believe about Reagan (his leadership has and will continue to bring prosperity and progress)?
- ✓ Who do you think the audience was (voting American public)?
- ✓ Did you notice the use of any rhetorical devices (anaphora, metaphor ["it's morning again in America . . . "], and rhetorical questions [e.g., "why would we ever want to return to 4 years ago?"]? Why do you think Reagan used these devices? Do you think they were effective?
- ✓ What did you notice about the voice of the speaker in the commercial (soothing, calm, measured pace)? How does it compare to the voice of the speaker in Johnson's Daisy Girl ad? Was Reagan speaking too quickly, too slowly, or just right? Think back to what Aristotle said about the way someone speaks (e.g., their rhythm and volume). Do you understand his point better after listening to this ad?

Some students may not be familiar with the presidency of Ronald Reagan. You may need to brief students on Reagan's opponent (Mondale) and some of Reagan's accomplishments, strengths (e.g., great communicator), weaknesses, etc. to contextualize the advertisement.

- Be sure students notice the phrase "it's morning again in America" was used literally in the ad (people going to work in the morning) and as a metaphor for hope and prosperity under Reagan's continued leadership.
- Discuss the voice of the speaker in the advertisement and its soothing, calm, well-paced delivery. This is important as students start to examine and discuss cadence, volume, and pitch. Consider asking students to take out the Preassessment and review the excerpt from Rhetoric that discusses these things.

9. Let students again work with a partner to complete another Handout 3.1. This advertisement and the Johnson advertisement are likely to generate considerable discussion among students, which provides an opportunity to monitor student comprehension and analysis of rhetorical appeals.
10. Ask students what they know about the 2008 competition between Hillary Clinton and Barack Obama for the nomination as candidate of the Democratic Party for president. You may have to spend a little time introducing this if students are unfamiliar with the Clinton versus Obama contest. Play the "3 a.m. at the White House" ad. After watching, pose the following questions:

- ✓ What are your general impressions of this political advertisement? What did you like/not like?
- ✓ Did you notice ethos (Clinton herself), pathos (beautiful children sleeping, something bad is happening in the world and your vote decides which President will respond), and/or logos (Clinton knows the military and world leaders, etc.)?
- ✓ What did the creator of the ad want the audience to do or believe about Clinton (she would be a better leader in dangerous times due to her experience on the world stage)?
- ✓ Who do you think the audience was (voting Democrats)?
- ✓ Did you notice the use of any rhetorical devices (e.g., anaphora, metaphor ["it's 3:00 a.m. and your children are safe and asleep . . . "] and rhetorical questions [e.g., "who do you want to answer the phone?"])? Why do you think Clinton used these devices? Do you think they were effective?
- ✓ What did you notice about the voice of the speaker in the commercial? How does it compare to the voice of the speaker in Johnson's "Daisy Girl" ad or Reagan's "Morning Again in America" ad?
- ✓ Which of the four political ads you saw today did you think was best and most effective? Why?

- Discuss the voice of the speaker in the Clinton advertisement. While it is quiet and well-paced, it has some urgency. Again, this observation is important as students start to examine and discuss cadence, volume and pitch.

Some students may not be familiar with this political competition. You may need to brief students to contextualize the advertisement. Be sure to note that Clinton tried to criticize Obama's lack of foreign policy experience and ability to lead the country in dangerous times.

11. Ask students to independently complete Handout 3.1. Be available to help any students who struggle with the independent activity and follow with whole-group discussion. Reinforce students' understanding that politicians purposefully use ethos, pathos, and logos in their advertisements along with common rhetorical devices.

You might have to caution students with very strong political positions to be respectful of divergent political and personal views, and to keep in mind that the point of the exercise is to explore the use of ethos, pathos, and logos in political advertising.

CLOSE

12. Remind students to put Handouts 2.1 and 3.1 back in their workbooks. Tell students that in the next lesson they will work in small groups to create their own corporate or political advertisement. Ask students to think about what type of advertisement they would like to create during the next lesson.

Help students identify a number of categories of advertisements for students to consider in order to create interest groups for the next lesson. For example, consider giving students the options of choosing (1) a presidential candidate (Democrat or Republican), (2) a sporting goods advertisement, (3) a charitable organization advertisement, (4) favorite food advertisement, or (5) a local political contest advertisement. These are only suggestions; these choices should be tailored to the interests of your students.

HOMEWORK

13. For homework, ask students to write down in their Student Workbook two possible advertisement options that they would be interested in creating with a small group of their peers.

PREPARATION: FOR NEXT LESSON

14. Read and provide feedback on students' Rhetoric Journals. For example, read journal entries and make notes about students' understanding of the particular rhetorical devices at this point in the unit. Provide notes to students to clarify any misunderstandings you note in the journals.

LESSON

5 Create Your Own Advertisement

MATERIALS

- ✓ Student journals
- ✓ Student workbooks
- ✓ Handout 1.1: Unit Preassessment
- ✓ Handouts 1.2A–C: Excerpts From *Rhetoric*
- ✓ Handout 5.1: Create an Advertisement Checklist (1 per group)

- Rhetoric is an art that can be systematically studied.
- Rhetoricians use a variety of appeals to persuade an audience.
- Rhetoric is vital to a healthy democracy.
- Understanding the interests and values of an audience is key to persuasion.

OBJECTIVES

Students will:

- ✓ generate ideas for persuasive speaking,
- ✓ express ideas clearly and persuasivcly,
- ✓ use clear reasons and relevant evidence,
- ✓ identify the values and interests of an audience,
- ✓ use rhetorical appeals and devices in their own speaking, and
- ✓ use appropriate cadence, volume, and pitch when trying to persuade an audience.

- Ethos
- Pathos
- Logos

SEQUENCE

WARM UP

1. Say: *It's time for our daily journal activity. Let's think about another time when someone—a friend, parent, coach, sibling, anyone—tried to persuade you to do or believe something. Try to remember as many details as you can about the event that comes into your mind. What did they want you to do or believe? Why? What did they say to persuade you? Were they successful at getting you to do or believe what they wanted? I will give you 30 seconds to quietly get a clear memory of that time with lots of details in your mind.*
2. After the 30 seconds are up, ask students to describe (in writing or a drawing) in their journal the time they remembered someone trying to persuade them to do or believe something. Let students know that they only have a couple of minutes to get down as many details as they can.

2E

By now students should be familiar with this daily activity. Students who struggle with written expression can continue to draw or bullet their rhetorical memories.

When students have finished, ask them to turn and share with a partner. Have the partner identify the appeal used by their partner. After students have shared their memories, remind students that it is important for them to understand the types of rhetorical appeals they find to be effective so that they can be aware of persuasion in their own lives.

INSTRUCTION: INTRODUCE CREATE AN ADVERTISEMENT ACTIVITY

You may have to engage in an inquiry process that leads students to these conclusions before moving on to the next component of this lesson.

3. Remind students that today they will create their own corporate or political advertisements in small groups, and then perform them for the class, but first it is important to revisit some of Aristotle's ideas from *Rhetoric*. Ask students to take out Handout 1.1: Unit Preassessment and refer to the excerpt from *Rhetoric*. Ask students to silently reread the excerpt.

When students have finished reading, engage the class in a discussion of what this excerpt means. Students should ultimately conclude that this excerpt addresses ethos and how a speaker can establish ethos. Students should also conclude that to be persuasive and appeal to an audience using ethos, it is important for the speaker to exhibit good sense, good moral character, and good will. Ask them to think back on the political advertisements from the last lesson for examples of ethos.

DISCUSSION: CADENCE ("RHYTHM"), VOLUME, AND PITCH

4. Ask students to take out Handout 1.2 from their workbooks (the excerpt from Aristotle's *Rhetoric*, Book III, Chapter 1 used in the Lesson 1 activity). Ask students to silently reread the excerpt.

When students have finished, engage them in a discussion of what this excerpt means. Students should ultimately conclude that this excerpt addresses the style or manner in which a speaker speaks, specifically their "rhythm" or cadence, volume, and pitch, and that how someone speaks is almost as important as what the speaker says.

5. Discuss the advertisements the class viewed in Lessons 3 and 4, specifically the way the speakers delivered their message. For example, compare the way Ronald Reagan spoke in "Moring Again in America" and how Johnson spoke in "Daisy Girl." Although the students discussed this in the last lesson, use this opportunity to define cadence, volume, and pitch for the students.
6. Tell students that when they create their own advertisement today, and in future rhetorical efforts, establishing their own ethos and using appropriate cadence, volume, and pitch will be important.
7. Explain to students that a speaker's cadence, volume, and pitch should "match" the purpose of the speech. For example, if a speaker wishes to reassure an audience, the cadence should be slow with emphasis on calming words, and the volume and pitch should be low. In contrast, if a speaker wishes to warn, the pitch and volume might be higher and the cadence more rapid.
8. Ask students to return Handouts 1.1 and 1.2 to their Student Workbooks. Remind students that they will refer back to these handouts throughout the unit.

To emphasize aligning the purpose of a speech with appropriate cadence, volume, and pitch, consider asking students to take out Handout 1.1 while using inappropriate cadence, volume, and pitch. For example, speak rapidly, loudly, and in a shrill manner when asking students to retrieve the handout from their workbooks. Then ask students what they noticed about the way you gave instructions, and whether it matched your request. This could be a segue into the conversation for this component of the lesson.

ACTIVITY: VOCAL WARM UP

9. Say to students: *Now we're going to stretch our tongues and lips and warm up our ability to enunciate with a tongue twister or two. Repeat*

the words "unique New York" as many times and as quickly as you can without any mispronunciations. After approximately 20–30 seconds, say to students: *Let's try another one. Repeat the words "black bug's blood" as many times and as quickly as you can without any mispronunciations.* Let students work on this tongue twister for approximately 20–30 seconds.

Remind students that good oral advocates need to exercise their voices and bodies to help them speak clearly. Invite students to stand up, close their eyes, and relax by taking deep breaths from their diaphragm (continue instructing students to breathe deeply until the room is quiet). Engage students in stretching for 2–3 minutes. For example, ask students to reach up to the ceiling as high as they can, and then slowly stretch down to their toes, to stretch from side to side with one arm over their head, to roll their shoulders and head around, etc.

- It is possible that some students may be reluctant or bashful public speakers. While recognizing those students' reluctance, place those students in interest groups with other students who will encourage and support all members of the group in speaking publicly.
- Some groups might want to get too "silly" in their advertisements. Rather than focusing on the criteria for the activity, they might focus on simply being funny or getting laughs. Remind students that while you want them to have fun you also expect them to take the activity seriously and be respectful of the advertisements of their classmates. Also remind them that being silly will compromise their ethos.

ACTIVITY: CREATE AN ADVERTISEMENT

Based on homework from the previous class, work with students to identify the types of advertisements that students wish to create (sports, cereal, political, public interest, etc.). Place students in groups of approximately 3–4 based on the interests they have expressed.

10. Briefly review the use of rhetorical appeals in the advertisements the class viewed over the last two lessons. Also review the use of rhetorical devices. Tell students that although they have not yet heard a wide variety of rhetorical devices, they will start to use them in this activity and will continue to be exposed to the use of rhetorical devices over the next several lessons.
11. Distribute Handout 5.1 (one per group). Tell students that each group will have 20 minutes to create an original advertisement of approximately 1 to 1 1/2 minutes. Their advertisement must reflect the use of ethos, logos, and/or pathos. Tell students that at least two of these appeals should be reflected in the advertisement. Their advertisement must also contain at least one rhetorical device. Each group should be able to identify the audience for the advertisement, as well as what they intend for that audience to do or believe as a result of the advertisement. Each student must have a speaking role in the advertisement. Particular attention should be given to cadence, volume, and pitch during the advertisement. Each group must complete Handout 5.1 as they develop

their advertisements to help ensure their group has satisfied each of the criteria for this activity.

12. Ask students if they have any questions about the Create an Advertisement activity. Tell them that this activity is supposed to be a fun way to explore and demonstrate understanding of the concepts learned in the unit so far. Acknowledge that 20 minutes of preparation may seem short, but tell students their objective is to be creative in a short period of time in order to demonstrate their developing understanding of the unit ideas and skills.
13. While students are preparing their advertisements, quietly visit with each group to ensure that they are on the right track. If necessary, provide guidance to groups to ensure they are satisfying the criteria for the activity. After approximately 20 minutes, tell students that it's time to present their advertisements!

Groups should be able to go to areas in the classroom where they have room to "act out" their advertisements. You may have to rearrange some desks/tables so students have room to create and perform.

ACTIVITY: ADVERTISEMENT PRESENTATIONS

14. Remind students that each group will have approximately 1 to 1.5 minutes to present its advertisement. Arrange a place in the classroom where groups will have sufficient room to present their advertisement. Also make sure all students who are not presenting can see the presentations. As each group comes to present, it should identify the product/person/organization it represents. Groups should also identify the audience they intend to persuade to do or believe something with their advertisement.
15. After each advertisement, ask the class to identify which rhetorical appeals and devices were used in the advertisement. You can also ask for a brief discussion of what was effective about the advertisement, or what changes could be suggested to make it more persuasive.

- Place group names in a "hat" and draw names to set the order.
- It might be necessary to remind students about class expectations for positive audience participation.

PREPARATION: FORMATIVE ASSESSMENT 2

16. Administer Performance Assessment 2 before Lesson 6. Have students respond to the following in their journals or as an exit card:
    - ✓ You just observed your classmates present their corporate or political advertisements. Of the advertisements you observed, what was the best example of a rhetorical appeal? Did it reflect the use of ethos, pathos, or logos?
    - ✓ Explain your response in detail. Was the use of this appeal appropriate for the intended audience of the advertisement?

17. **Using the assessment data:** Use student responses to Formative Assessment 2 and the advertisement activity to monitor progress and to get an idea of who may be struggling with rhetorical appeals in adver-

tising and who may need more of a challenge. This will help you make informed decisions about grouping and the need for additional modeling or mini-lessons in future lessons.

HOMEWORK

18. Tell students that they will continue to examine rhetoric during the next lesson, but they will do so by viewing and analyzing political speeches and eulogies of famous people. Make sure students know what *eulogy* means. Ask students to speak to a parent, adult, or guardian about a political speech or eulogy the adult recalls and whether ethos, pathos, or logos were used.

PREPARATION: FOR NEXT LESSON

19. Make notes about students' developing understanding at this point in the unit. Return and provide feedback in Student Journals. If necessary, meet with students who are struggling with the concepts to date to clarify misunderstandings.

Name: ______________________________ **Date:** ______________

HANDOUT 5.1

CREATE AN ADVERTISEMENT CHECKLIST

Directions: Answer the following questions about your advertisement. Use a separate sheet of paper if necessary.

1. What type of advertisement will your group create? In other words, what are you advertising?

2. Who is your audience?

3. What do you want your audience to do or believe?

4. What rhetorical appeals did you use? Why did you choose these appeals? Be specific.

HANDOUT 5.1, CONTINUED

5. Did you establish ethos? How did you establish goodwill and good moral character?

6. Did you use appropriate cadence, volume, and pitch?

7. What rhetorical device(s) did you use? Why did choose these? Be specific.

8. Did everyone in your group have a speaking role?

LESSON

6 Epideictic Rhetoric

MATERIALS

- ✓ Student journals
- ✓ Student workbooks
- ✓ Political speeches and famous eulogies (available on YouTube):
  - Robert Kennedy on Martin Luther King Jr.'s death (available at https://www.youtube.com/watch?v=GoKzCff8Zbs)
  - Maya Angelou eulogizes Coretta Scott King (available at https://www.youtube.com/watch?v=otGXTryeY6w)
  - Lou Gehrig's July 4th farewell to baseball address (available at https://www.youtube.com/watch?v=3oW1RuGqw7g)
- ✓ Handout 3.1: Rhetorical Appeal and Device Identifier (three copies per student)
- ✓ Handout 6.1A: Excerpts from Aristotle's *Rhetoric*, Book I: Chapter 3 (hardest)
- ✓ Handout 6.1B: Excerpts from Aristotle's *Rhetoric*, Book I: Chapter 3 (on-level)
- ✓ Handout 6.1C: Excerpts from Aristotle's *Rhetoric*, Book I: Chapter 3 (easiest)

- Rhetoric is an art that can be systematically studied.
- Rhetoricians use a variety of appeals to persuade an audience.
- Rhetoric is vital to a healthy democracy.
- The use of logic and reason, rather than force, to persuade others is a uniquely human capacity.
- Rhetoric can be used to promote or injure the common good.
- Understanding the interests and values of an audience is key to persuasion.

OBJECTIVES

Students will:

- ✓ build rhetoric vocabulary;
- ✓ identify epideictic speech;
- ✓ identify rhetorical appeals and devices used by a speaker;
- ✓ analyze rhetorical appeals and devices used by a speaker;
- ✓ identify values and interests of an audience;
- ✓ participate as knowledgeable, reflective, and critical members of a rhetorical community; and
- ✓ analyze cadence, volume, and pitch.

- Epideictic rhetoric
- Political rhetoric
- Forensic rhetoric

SEQUENCE

WARM UP

1. Say: *We're going to get started on our daily rhetoric journal reflection. Close your eyes and think about a time when you tried to persuade someone—a friend, parent, coach, sibling, anyone—to do or believe something. Try to remember as many details as you can about the event that comes into your mind. What did you want them to do or believe? Why? What did you say to persuade them? Why did you choose the words you used? Did you use ethos, pathos, or logos? Were you successful—did you get the person to do or believe what you wanted? I will give you 30 seconds to quietly get a clear memory of that time with lots of details in your mind.*

After the 30 seconds are up, ask students to describe (in writing or a drawing) in their journal the time they remembered trying to persuade someone to do or believe something. Remind students that they only have a couple of minutes to get down as many details as they can.

2. After writing, ask students to turn to their neighbor and share their memories. Ask partners to identify the rhetorical appeal used by their partners.

INSTRUCTION: EPIDEICTIC RHETORIC

Distribute Handout 6.1 (levels A, B, and C, based on unit preassessment). These handouts contain an excerpt of Aristotle's *Rhetoric*, Book I, Ch. 3, specifically sections about epideictic (ceremonial), political (deliberative), and forensic speech.

3. Tell students that they will be reading more excerpts from Aristotle's *Rhetoric*. Explain that Aristotle said that there are three types of rhetoric, and that each has a different and specific purpose. Let students know they should try to determine the three types of rhetoric and the purpose for each. Let the students know that this excerpt is very challenging, but that they should persist in working toward an understanding of the text. Ask students to read silently and independently.
4. When students have finished reading, ask them to state the purpose of political speech in their own words. Through discussion, students should come to understand that the purpose of political speech is to persuade the audience to do something in the future because it will promote good, or to not do something in the future that will cause harm. They are often called public policy speeches. Ask the students to discriminate between a political speech of a candidate for office and a political speech that persuades an audience to do or not do something. Ask them to give examples. If they struggle to come up with an example, consider referring back to the SPCA advertisement or select a public service advertisement from your community to discuss.
5. Next, ask students to state the purpose of forensic speech in their own words. Through discussion, students should come to understand that the purpose of forensic speech is to persuade the audience to judge something that happened in the past, such as in a trial.
6. Next, ask students to state the purpose of ceremonial oratory of display, otherwise known as epideictic speech. Through discussion, students should come to understand that the purpose of epideictic speech is to inspire people. It is also used to honor someone today, although one can recall a person's past in honoring them. Finally, epideictic speech is also used to unify a group of people and to provide hope or catharsis in times of crisis.
7. Now, explain to students that they're going to watch some examples of exemplary epideictic speeches. Tell students they should be thinking about what rhetorical appeals are being used, what the speaker is

- As with the readiness level groups formed in Lesson 1, it is possible that not all three versions of the selected excerpt from *Rhetoric* will be necessary.
- If it appears from student feedback that the excerpt was too challenging for many to decipher, read the version you believe to be most appropriate based on student readiness aloud with emphasis on important words and phrases relating to epideictic (ceremonial), political (deliberative), and forensic forms of speech, stopping throughout the reading to be sure students comprehend at appropriate and important points.

trying to persuade the audience to do or believe, and who the audience members are. Distribute Handout 3.1. Explain to students that they will use this worksheet to write their reflections and observations about the rhetorical appeals and devices used by the speakers.

The YouTube clips selected for this lesson exemplify epideictic speech. You might select different speeches and/or eulogies based on the interests and level of understanding of your students. However, you should select epideictic speeches that also clearly use identifiable rhetorical appeals.

2E

Some of the speeches students will watch in this lesson are also available in written form at http://www.tonguetiedamerica.com. You might wish to make copies of the speeches for students to use and have available as a supplement to the videos. This would be helpful to students with auditory processing challenges.

8. Ask students to carefully watch and listen to Robert Kennedy's speech. Ask students to think about what Kennedy is trying to get his audience to do or believe (to honor King and to remain peaceful in a time of crisis).

- Ask them to watch out for the use of rhetorical appeals and devices, and to take notes on the back of their Rhetorical Appeals and Devices Worksheet.
- Some (or all) students could also read the speech to supplement their comprehension.

9. After watching, pose the following questions:
   - ✓ What is Kennedy trying to make the audience believe or do? How did he try to accomplish this?
   - ✓ Did Kennedy use pathos, logos, or ethos in his speech? Did he use rhetorical devices (e.g., parallelism, metaphor, anaphora, etc.)? Where? How? Do you think they were effective?
   - ✓ Who is the audience?
   - ✓ Why do you think this is called one of the greatest epideictic speeches? What do you think of this speech? How did it make you feel?
   - ✓ How would you describe Kennedy's cadence, volume, and pitch? Was Kennedy's cadence, volume, and pitch appropriate for the occasion of his speech?
   - ✓ Do you think Kennedy skillfully convinced the audience to avoid the use of violence and force?

10. Following this discussion, work together with the students to complete Handout 3.1. As students are just beginning to recognize and identify rhetorical devices, this might take more explanation. Check for understanding with a brief follow-up conversation with students sharing responses with rationales for their answers.

- You will likely have to explain to students the historical context in which this speech took place. Specifically, tell students that New York Senator (and brother of assassinated President John Kennedy) Robert Kennedy was running to be the Democratic nominee for President in 1968. At a campaign stop in Indianapolis, IN, Kennedy received word that Martin Luther King Jr.—the civil rights leader—had been assassinated. Although police had warned him that people might riot, Kennedy felt he had to tell the mixed-race crowd about this death. With very little time to prepare the speech, he delivered the speech without any drafts or prewritten words. This speech was delivered on a back of a flatbed truck. Although all major cities had riots, Indianapolis remained calm after Kennedy's speech. Sixty-three days after this speech, Kennedy was assassinated.
- It is important to students to recognize that the speakers today establish ethos by virtue of their relationships with the audience and their own personal fame, as well as pathos to draw on the sympathy and respect from the audience. Logos can also be found, particularly in Kennedy's speech. It is important that students be able to identify how and where each of these appeals are used.

11. Next, ask students if they've ever been to a funeral, or watched a funeral on television or in a movie. Ask students if they can define *eulogy*. To those students who have attended or watched a funeral, ask if they remember the eulogy. Ask what words were used and what they think the purpose of the eulogy was, who they think would be the best person to deliver a eulogy (relatives, friends, etc.), and if there are any traits someone delivering a eulogy should possess. Ask students to carefully watch and listen to Maya Angelou's eulogy of Coretta Scott King. Ask students to think about what Angelou is trying to get her audience to do or believe (to commemorate a great figure in American history and to comfort the grieving). Ask them to watch for the use of rhetorical appeals and devices, and to take notes on Handout 3.1 if necessary. After watching, pose the following questions:
    - ✓ What do you think Angelou's relationship was with King? Does she sound like she is grieving or celebrating?
    - ✓ What is Angelou trying to make the audience believe or do? How did she try to accomplish this?
    - ✓ Did Angelou use pathos, logos, or ethos—or a combination—in her speech? Did she use rhetorical devices (e.g., anaphora, alliteration,

euphemism, metaphor, etc.)? Where? How? Do you think they were effective?

- ✓ Who is the audience? Why do you think this is called a great epideictic speech? What do you think of this speech? How did it make you feel?
- ✓ How would you describe Angelou's cadence, volume, and pitch? Was Angelou's cadence, volume, and pitch appropriate for the occasion of her speech?
- ✓ What made her an appropriate person to deliver the eulogy?
- ✓ What did you think about her singing a spiritual at the beginning of her eulogy? Why do you think she did that?

You will likely have to explain to students the historical context in which this speech took place. Specifically, students should understand that Coretta Scott King was the wife of Martin Luther King Jr., and was a deeply respected civil rights figure in her own right. More than 10,000 people, including many world leaders, attended her 2006 funeral. You should also remind students that Maya Angelou was a famous American writer and poet who recited a poem at the 1993 inauguration of President Clinton.

Following this discussion, place students in pairs or small groups. Ask them to work in their pairs/small groups to complete Handout 3.1. As students discuss their answers, walk through the classroom to monitor their comprehension of the task. Check for overall class understanding with a brief follow-up conversation that reviews answers on the worksheets.

12. Ask students to listen carefully to Lou Gehrig's Farewell to Baseball Address. Explain to the students that there is audio of the speech but not a video of the entire speech (although there are some photographs). After watching, pose the following questions to the students:
    - ✓ What is Lou Gehrig trying to make you believe or do? How did he try to accomplish this?
    - ✓ Does Lou Gehrig seem to feel sorry for himself in this speech? How would you feel if you were diagnosed with a deadly cancer?
    - ✓ How did you feel listening to Gehrig make his speech? Did Lou Gehrig use pathos, logos, or ethos—or a combination of them—in his speech? Where? How?
    - ✓ Did he use rhetorical devices in his speech (e.g., euphemism, hyperbole, conduplicatio, etc.)? Where? Which ones?
    - ✓ Who is the audience?
    - ✓ What do you think of this speech? Why do you think it is called a great epideictic speech? (Be sure students understand that epideic-

tic rhetoric is not limited to eulogizing, but rather it applies to all speeches meant to inspire and honor a person or cause.)

You may have to explain that Lou Gehrig was a beloved Hall of Fame baseball legend, who played for the New York Yankees in the 1930s. He was diagnosed with a rare form of cancer that would make his body deteriorate. Upon his diagnosis, he announced his retirement from the Yankees and made what is often called the most famous sports speech ever.

Following this discussion, place students in pairs or small groups. Ask them to work in their pairs/small groups to complete Handout 3.1. As students discuss their answers, walk through the classroom to monitor their comprehension of the task. Check for overall class understanding with a brief follow-up conversation that reviews answers on the worksheets. Ask students to put completed copies of Handout 3.1 in their workbooks.

CLOSE

13. Tell students that you will continue to examine famous speeches during the next lesson. Explain that the focus of the next lesson is political rather than epideictic rhetoric.

PREPARATION: FOR NEXT LESSON

14. Read student journal responses and make notes about students' developing understandings at this point in the unit. In addition, review and provide feedback on students' Rhetorical Appeals and Devices Identifier worksheets (Handout 3.1). If necessary, meet with students who are struggling with the concepts to date to clarify misunderstandings.

HANDOUT 6.1A

EXCERPTS FROM ARISTOTLE'S *RHETORIC*, BOOK 1: CHAPTER 3

Rhetoric falls into three divisions, determined by the three classes of listeners to speeches. For of the three elements in speech-making—speaker, subject, and person addressed—it is the last one, the hearer, that determines the speech's end and object. The hearer must be either a judge, with a decision to make about things past or future, or an observer. A member of the assembly decides about future events, a juryman about past events: while those who merely decide on the orator's skill are observers. From this it follows that there are three divisions of oratory—(1) political, (2) forensic, and (3) the ceremonial oratory of display.

Political speaking urges us either to do or not to do something . . . . Forensic speaking either attacks or defends somebody: one or other of these two things must always be done by the parties in a case. The ceremonial oratory of display either praises or censures somebody. These three kinds of rhetoric refer to three different kinds of time. The political orator is concerned with the future: it is about things to be done hereafter that he advises, for or against. The party in a case at law is concerned with the past; one man accuses the other, and the other defends himself, with reference to things already done. The ceremonial orator is, properly speaking, concerned with the present, since all men praise or blame in view of the state of things existing at the time, though they often find it useful also to recall the past and to make guesses at the future.

Rhetoric has three distinct ends in view, one for each of its three kinds. The political orator aims at establishing the expediency or the harmfulness of a proposed course of action; if he urges its acceptance, he does so on the ground that it will do good; if he urges its rejection, he does so on the ground that it will do harm; and all other points, such as whether the proposal is just or unjust, honourable or dishonourable, he brings in as subsidiary and relative to this main consideration. Parties in a law-case aim at establishing the justice or injustice of some action, and they too bring in all other points as subsidiary and relative to this one. Those who praise or attack a man aim at proving him worthy of honour or the reverse, and they too treat all other considerations with reference to this one.

HANDOUT 6.1B

EXCERPTS FROM ARISTOTLE'S *RHETORIC*, BOOK 1: CHAPTER 3

[**There are three kinds of rhetoric: (1) political, (2) forensic, and (3) the ceremonial oratory of display**.]

Political speaking urges us either to do or not to do something.... Forensic speaking either attacks or defends somebody . . . . The ceremonial oratory of display either praises or censures somebody. These three kinds of rhetoric refer to three different kinds of time. The **political orator** is concerned with the **future**: it is about things to be done hereafter that he advises, for or against. The party in a case at law [**forensic orator**] is concerned with the **past**; one man accuses the other, and the other defends himself, with reference to things already done. The **ceremonial orator** is . . . concerned with the **present**, since all men praise or blame in view of the state of things existing at the time . . . .

Rhetoric has three distinct ends in view, one for each of its three kinds. The political orator aims at establishing the expediency or the harmfulness of a proposed course of action; if he urges its acceptance, he does so on the ground that it will do good; if he urges its rejection, he does so on the ground that it will do harm . . . . Parties in a law-case aim at establishing the justice or injustice of some action . . . . Those who praise or attack a man aim at proving him worthy of honour or the reverse . . . .

HANDOUT 6.1C

EXCERPTS FROM ARISTOTLE'S *RHETORIC*, BOOK 1: CHAPTER 3

[There are three kinds of rhetoric: (1) political, (2) forensic, and (3) the ceremonial oratory of display.]

Political speaking urges us either to do or not to do something.... Forensic speaking either attacks or defends somebody . . . . The ceremonial oratory of display either praises or censures somebody. These three kinds of rhetoric refer to three different kinds of time. The **political orator** is concerned with the **future**: it is about things to be done hereafter that he advises, for or against. The party in a case at law [**forensic orator**] is concerned with the **past**; one man accuses the other, and the other defends himself, with reference to things already done. The **ceremonial orator** is . . . concerned with the **present**, since all men praise or blame in view of the state of things existing at the time . . . .

Rhetoric has three distinct ends in view, one for each of its three kinds. The political orator aims at establishing the expediency or the harmfulness of a proposed course of action; if he urges its acceptance, he does so on the ground that it will do good; if he urges its rejection, he does so on the ground that it will do harm . . . . Parties in a law-case aim at establishing the justice or injustice of some action . . . . Those who praise or attack a man aim at proving him worthy of honour or the reverse . . . .

LESSON

7 Deliberative (Political) Rhetoric

MATERIALS

- ✓ Student journals
- ✓ Student workbooks
- ✓ Famous political speeches (available on YouTube):
  - Kerry Washington performing Sojourner Truth's "Ain't I A Woman" Speech (available at https://www.youtube.com/watch?v=yq3AYiRT4no)
  - Congresswoman Barbara Jordan, Statement on the Articles of Impeachment, delivered July 25, 1974, before the House Judiciary Committee (available at https://www.youtube.com/watch?v=CDcYiyF5eLc)

- ✓ Handout 3.1: Rhetorical Appeals and Devices Identifier (two copies per student)
- ✓ Handouts 6.1A–C: Excerpts from Aristotle's *Rhetoric*, Book I: Chapter 3

- Rhetoric is an art that can be systematically studied.
- Rhetoricians use a variety of appeals to persuade an audience.
- Understanding the interests and values of an audience is key to persuasion.
- Rhetoric is vital to a healthy democracy.
- The use of logic and reason, rather than force, to persuade others is a uniquely human capacity.
- Rhetoric can be used to promote or injure the common good.

OBJECTIVES

Students will:

- ✓ build rhetoric vocabulary;
- ✓ identify deliberative (political) and forensic rhetoric;
- ✓ identify rhetorical appeals and devices used by a speaker;
- ✓ analyze rhetorical appeals and devices used by a speaker;

- ✓ identify values and interests of an audience;
- ✓ participate as knowledgeable, reflective, and critical members of a rhetorical community; and
- ✓ analyze cadence, volume, and pitch.

- Deliberative rhetoric

SEQUENCE

WARM UP

1. Say: *We're going to get started on our daily rhetoric journal reflection. Close your eyes and think about a time when you listened to a speech that inspired you. Try to remember as many details as you can about the event that comes into your mind. What did the speaker want you to do or believe? What did the speaker say to inspire you? What words did the speaker use? Why do you think the speaker choose the words he or she used? Did the speaker use ethos, pathos, and/or logos? I will give you 30 seconds to quietly get a clear memory of that time with lots of details in your mind.*

After the 30 seconds are up, ask students to describe (in writing or a drawing) in their journal the time they listened to a speech that inspired them. Remind students that they only have a couple of minutes to get down as many details as they can. Ask students to turn to their neighbor and share their memories. Ask students to identify the rhetorical appeal reflected in the memory of his or her partner.

INSTRUCTION: DELIBERATIVE RHETORIC

2. Tell students that today they will continue to examine political and forensic rhetoric that was described in Aristotle's *Rhetoric*. Explain that "political" speech is also referred to as "deliberative." Remind students that they examined examples of epideictic rhetoric in the last lesson. Explain that today they will examine political and forensic rhetorical exemplars. Tell students to reread the excerpts from Aristotle's *Rhetoric*, Book I: Chapter 3 (Handout 6.1, from their workbooks) related to epideictic (ceremonial), political, and forensic speech.

- Ask students if they have any questions about the epideictic speeches they heard in the last lesson. You might have to clarify with students the fact that politicians can make epideictic speeches.
- Remind students that the purpose of political speech is to persuade the audience to do something in the future because it will promote the public good or to avoid doing something in the future that will cause harm. These speeches are often public policy speeches. Remind students that people other than politicians can make political speeches. Ask students to give an example of a political speech they have heard. Use these responses to judge students' understanding. If they cannot give an example, provide one from your experience.
- Remind students that the purpose of forensic speech is to persuade the audience to do judge something that happened in the past. It might be helpful to explain that this is the type of speech they would see in closing arguments at a trial when judging someone's guilt or innocence or reaching a verdict. Ask students to give an example from a forensic speech they have heard on television or have seen in a movie. If they cannot give an example, provide one from a film or television series that is current and popular.

2E

Some students who struggle with organization may need help with maintaining their workbooks. Some of these students may also require new copies of Aristotle's *Rhetoric*, Book I: Chapter 3 if they have misplaced their original copies.

The YouTube clips selected for this lesson exemplify political, deliberative speech. You might select different speeches and/or eulogies based on the interests of your students. However, you should select deliberative speeches that also use identifiable rhetorical appeals.

3. Explain to students that they are going to watch some examples of exemplary political and deliberative speeches. Tell students they should be thinking about what rhetorical appeals are being used, what the speaker is trying to persuade the audience to do or believe, and who the audience members are. Distribute three copies of Handout 3.1 to each student. Explain to students that they will use this worksheet to write their reflections and observations about the rhetorical appeals and devices used by the speakers.

2E

The speeches students will watch in this lesson are also available in written form at http://www.tonguetiedamerica.com. You might wish to make copies of the speeches for students to use and have available as a supplement to the videos. Having the written text of these speeches may be helpful to students with deficits in auditory processing.

4. Ask students to carefully watch and listen to Kerry Washington performing Sojourner Truth's "Ain't I A Woman" Speech. You might also provide written copies of the speech to aid student comprehension.

Ask students to think about what Truth is trying to get her audience to do or believe (to give women the right to vote). Ask them to watch for the use of rhetorical appeals and devices, and to take notes on the back of Handout 3.1 as they listen to the speech.

5. After watching, pose the following questions:
   - ✓ What is Truth trying to make the audience believe or do (give women the right to vote)? How did she try to accomplish this?
   - ✓ Did Truth use pathos (e.g., bible references), logos (e.g., the types of work she has done), or ethos (e.g., "and ain't I a woman?") in her speech? Did she use rhetorical devices? Where? Which one(s)? How do you think the rhetorical devices made the speech more persuasive?
   - ✓ Who is the audience?
   - ✓ Why do you think this is called one of the greatest political speeches in our history? What do you think of this speech? How did it make you feel? Were you persuaded? Of what? Why?

6. Following this discussion, work together with the students to complete Handout 3.1. Alternatively, let students complete the worksheet independently or in pairs of their choice. As students continue to build their recognition of rhetorical devices, they may need additional support and explanation. Check for understanding with a brief follow-up conversation of student responses.

You will likely have to explain to students the historical context in which this speech took place. Specifically, tell students that Sojourner Truth was an emancipated slave and abolitionist from New York who delivered this speech in 1851 at the Women's Rights Convention in Akron, OH. At that time, it was very rare for African American women to speak before an audience consisting mostly of White, privileged women. While historical accounts of the speech vary, a woman attending the convention named Francis Gage first published the version the students will hear in 1863.

7. Introduce Congresswoman Barbara Jordan's Statement on the Articles of Impeachment, delivered July 25, 1974, before the House Judiciary Committee. Because this is a lengthy speech, it is recommended that students have a written version of the speech as well. Ask students to think about what Jordan is trying to get her audience—other members of Congress—to do or believe (impeach President Nixon). Ask them to

watch for the use of rhetorical appeals and devices, and to take notes on the back of their Rhetorical Appeals and Devices Worksheet as they listen to the speech. After watching, pose the following questions:

- ✓ What is Jordan trying to make the audience believe or do? How did she try to accomplish this?
- ✓ Did Jordan use pathos (e.g., noting the historically recent citizenship of African Americans), logos (e.g., Constitutional text, the evidence against Nixon), or ethos (e.g., "We the people") in her speech?
- ✓ Did she use rhetorical devices? Where ("It is reason, and not passion, which must guide or deliberations, guide or debate, and guide our decision")? Which one(s)? How do you think the rhetorical devices made the speech more persuasive?
- ✓ Who is the audience?
- ✓ Why do you think this is called one of the greatest political speeches in our history? What do you think of this speech? How did it make you feel? Were you persuaded? Of what? Why?

You will likely have to explain to students the historical context in which this speech took place. Specifically, tell students that Barbara Jordan was an African American Freshman United States Congresswoman when the House Judiciary Committee considered Articles of Impeachment against President Nixon. She was also the first African American woman elected to Congress from a Southern state.

8. Following this discussion, let students work with a student of their choice to complete Handout 3.1. As students continue to build their recognition of rhetorical devices, they may need additional support and explanation. Check for understanding with a brief follow-up conversation of student responses.

LESSON

8 Forensic Rhetoric

MATERIALS

- ✓ Student journals
- ✓ Student workbooks
- ✓ Atticus Finch's closing argument from *To Kill a Mockingbird* (available at https://www.youtube.com/watch?v=8MmtVx1A8BA)
- ✓ Handout 3.1: Rhetorical Appeals and Devices Identifier (two copies per student)
- ✓ Handouts 6.1A–C: Excerpts From Aristotle's *Rhetoric*, Book 1: Chapter 3

- Rhetoric is an art that can be systematically studied.
- Rhetoricians use a variety of appeals to persuade an audience.
- Understanding the interests and values of an audience is key to persuasion.
- Rhetoric is vital to a healthy democracy.
- The use of logic and reason, rather than force, to persuade others is a uniquely human capacity.
- Rhetoric can be used to promote or injure the common good.

OBJECTIVES

Students will:

- ✓ build rhetoric vocabulary;
- ✓ identify deliberative (political) and forensic rhetoric;
- ✓ identify rhetorical appeals and devices used by a speaker;
- ✓ analyze rhetorical appeals and devices used by a speaker;
- ✓ identify values and interests of an audience;
- ✓ participate as knowledgeable, reflective, and critical members of a rhetorical community; and
- ✓ analyze cadence, volume, and pitch.

- Deliberative or political rhetoric
- Forensic rhetoric

SEQUENCE

WARM UP

1. Say: *We're going to get started on our daily rhetoric journal reflection. Close your eyes and think about a time when you listened to a speech that did not inspire you. Try to remember as many details as you can about the event that comes into your mind. What did the speaker want you to do or believe? What did the speaker say to inspire you? What words did the speaker use? Why do you think the speaker choose the words he or she used? Did the speaker use ethos, pathos, and/or logos? Why do you think the speech failed to inspire you to do or believe something? What could the speaker have done differently? I will give you 30 seconds to quietly get a clear memory of that time with lots of details in your mind.*

After the 30 seconds are up, ask students to describe (in writing or a drawing) in their journal the time they listened to a speech that failed to inspire them. Remind students know that they only have a couple of minutes to get down as many details as they can.

2. Ask students to turn to their neighbor and share their memories. Ask students to identify the rhetorical appeal reflected in the memory of his or her partner.

INSTRUCTION: EPIDEICTIC SPEECH

3. Tell students that today they will continue to examine political and forensic rhetoric that was described in Aristotle's *Rhetoric*. Remind students that they examined examples of political rhetoric in the last lesson. Explain that today they will examine forensic rhetoric. Tell students to reread Handout 6.1.

- Ask students if they have any questions about the political (deliberative) speeches they heard in the last lesson. You might have to clarify with students the fact that nonpoliticians like Sojourner Truth can make political speeches.
- Remind students that the purpose of forensic speech is to persuade the audience to judge something that happened in the past. It might be helpful to explain that this is the type of speech they would see in closing arguments at a trial when judging someone's guilt or innocence or reaching a verdict. Ask students if they can give an example of forensic speech they have heard on television or have seen in a movie. If they cannot give an example, provide one from a film or television series that is current and popular.

4. Explain to students that they are going to watch an example of exemplary forensic speech. Tell students they should be thinking about what rhetorical appeals are being used, what the speaker is trying to persuade the audience to do or believe, and who the audience members are. Distribute Handout 3.1. Explain to students that they will continue to use this worksheet to write their reflections and observations about the rhetorical appeals and devices used by the speakers.
5. Ask students to carefully watch and listen to Atticus Finch's closing argument from the movie *To Kill a Mockingbird*. Ask students to think about what Finch is trying to get the jury to do or believe (to acquit Tom Robinson and find he is innocent). Ask them to watch for the use of rhetorical appeals and devices, and to take notes on the back of Handout 3.1 as they listen to the closing argument.

If students are not familiar with *To Kill a Mockingbird*, explain that Atticus Finch is a small town lawyer from Alabama defending an African American man—Tom Robinson—wrongly accused of violence against a White woman. Explain in a way that is appropriate for your students some of the issues of racial discrimination in the South during the time of the book's setting, and the difficulties African Americans had being treated fairly in courts of law.

Some teachers may find the underlying themes from *To Kill a Mockingbird* to be too mature for their students. In that case, consider using a court scene from a different movie where political/forensic speech is used. For example, you could use the Ministry of Magic disciplinary hearing scene from the movie *Harry Potter and the Order of the Phoenix*.

6. After watching, pose the following questions:
   - ✓ What is Finch trying to make the jury believe or do (that Tom Robinson was not guilty and should be acquitted)? How did he try to accomplish this?
   - ✓ Did Finch use pathos (e.g., describing his pity for Mayella Ewell), logos (e.g., describing the evidence exonerating Tom Robinson), or ethos (e.g., invoking the honor of court proceedings and God) in his closing argument?
   - ✓ What rhetorical devices did he use? Where? Which one (metaphor)? How do you think the rhetorical devices made the closing argument more persuasive?
   - ✓ Why do you think this is called one of the greatest closing arguments in movie history?
   - ✓ What do you think of this closing argument? How did it make you feel? Were you persuaded? Of what? Why?

CLOSE

7. Following this discussion, ask students to complete independently Handout 3.1. Check for understanding with a brief follow-up conversation of student responses. Ask students to place the completed handout in their workbooks.

8. This is a good time to check with students to ensure their comprehension of the three types of rhetoric. It would also be a good time to check in with students to make sure they are developing the knowledge and skills of the unit as they get closer to the creation of their own rhetorical endeavors.

HOMEWORK

9. Tell students that they will have the opportunity to create independently a short epideictic, political, or forensic speech during the next lesson. The speech should be 2–3 minutes long. For homework, ask students to think about what type of speech they would like to create.

If you are concerned about the potential for inappropriate topic selections, consider asking students to identify their choices in writing for homework. This will provide the opportunity to quickly review student selections and to engage students in selecting appropriate substitute selections as necessary.

Discuss a variety of options that will interest the students. For example, if they choose to do a eulogy, tell students they can create a eulogy about a favorite character from fiction, a favorite historical figure, or even a friend or family member. If they choose to do a political speech, they can speak about an issue in their school, family, or community that is personally important.

PREPARATION: FOR NEXT LESSON

10. Continue to read student journal responses and make notes about students' developing understandings at this point in the unit. In addition, review and provide feedback on Handout 3.1. If necessary, meet with students who are struggling with the concepts to clarify misunderstandings before the next lesson.

LESSON

9 Create Your Own Epideictic, Forensic, or Political Speech

MATERIALS

- ✓ Student journals
- ✓ Student workbooks
- ✓ Handout 9.1: Create a Speech Checklist

- Rhetoric is an art that can be systematically studied.
- Rhetoricians use a variety of appeals to persuade an audience.
- Rhetoric is vital to a healthy democracy.
- Understanding the interests and values of an audience is key to persuasion.

OBJECTIVES

Students will:

- ✓ generate ideas for persuasive speaking,
- ✓ express ideas clearly and persuasively,
- ✓ use clear reasons and relevant evidence,
- ✓ identify the values and interests of an audience,
- ✓ use rhetorical appeals and devices in their own speaking, and
- ✓ use appropriate cadence, volume, and pitch when trying to persuade an audience.

- Ethos
- Pathos
- Logos
- Epideictic rhetoric
- Forensic rhetoric
- Political rhetoric

SEQUENCE

WARM UP

1. Say: *It's time for our daily journal reflection. We have listened to several examples of excellent rhetoric including commercial and political advertisements, as well as epideictic, forensic, and political speeches. For today's journal activity, I'd like you to think about which of the rhetorical exemplars or videos we have heard so far that you found to be the most persuasive. Try to remember as many details as you can about the rhetorical exemplar that comes into your mind. What was most persuasive about the speech or advertisement? What did you like about it? What rhetorical appeal(s) were used effectively? Were there also effective rhetorical devices in the exemplar? I will give you 30 seconds to quietly get a clear memory of that rhetorical exemplar with lots of details in your mind.*

After the 30 seconds are up, ask students to describe in their journals (in writing or a drawing) which rhetorical exemplar each found to be the most persuasive. Remind students that they only have a couple of minutes to get down as many details as possible.

When students have finished, ask them to turn and share their choices with their chair neighbor. Have partners identify the rhetorical appeal(s) and device(s) used. After pairs have shared, take a class poll to see which rhetorical exemplar was selected by the greatest number of students. As a class, determine what was most appealing and persuasive about the exemplar. Let students know that you will come back to this question as a class and will discuss it more fully in subsequent lessons.

Students should have copies of the excerpts from Aristotle's *Rhetoric* available in their workbook.

INSTRUCTION: REVISIT ARISTOTLE'S IDEAS

2. Tell students that they will create their own political or epideictic speech to perform for the class, but first it is important to revisit some of Aristotle's ideas from *Rhetoric*. Ask students to take Handout 6.1 from their workbooks. Ask students to silently reread the excerpts.

When students have finished reading, engage the class in a review of what these excerpts mean. Students should ultimately recall that the purpose of deliberative or political speech is to persuade someone to do something in the future, forensic speech is to persuade an audience about what happened in the past, whereas the purpose of epideictic speech is to inspire or honor someone admired by an audience. You should also remind students that to be persuasive a speaker must always develop ethos by exhibiting good sense, good moral character, and goodwill toward the audience.

3. Ask students to take out Handout 1.1, which is the excerpt from Aristotle's *Rhetoric*, Book III, Chapter 1, addressing the need to use appropriate volume, cadence, and pitch. Ask students to silently review the excerpt.

When students have finished reading, engage the class in a brief review of what that excerpt means. Students should ultimately remember that this excerpt addresses the style or manner in which a speaker speaks, specifically their cadence, volume, and pitch, and that the way someone sounds when he or she speaks is almost as important as what the speaker says. Ask students to demonstrate good use of pitch, cadence, and volume.

4. Discuss the speeches the class viewed in Lessons 6 through 8, specifically the way each speaker delivered his or her message. For example, compare the way Maya Angelou spoke at Coretta Scott King's funeral to how Kennedy spoke following the death of Martin Luther King Jr. and how Atticus Finch delivered his closing argument.
5. Tell students that when they create their own speech today, and in their future rhetorical endeavors, establishing ethos and using appropriate cadence, volume, and pitch will be important. Ask students to return the handouts to their workbooks, but remind them that they may refer back to them in subsequent activities.

ACTIVITY: VOCAL WARM UP

Remind students that good oral advocates need to exercise their voices and bodies to help them speak clearly. Invite students to stand up, close their eyes, and relax by taking deep breaths from their diaphragm (continue instructing students to breathe deeply until the room is quiet). Engage students in stretching for 2–3 minutes. For example, ask students to reach up to the ceiling as high as they can, and then slowly stretch down to their toes, to stretch from side to side with one arm over their head, to roll their shoulders and head around, etc.

To vary this activity, consider allowing a student or group of students to lead the class in this and future vocal warm up exercises. Also, consider allowing students to use different stretching activities that they may have used in physical education classes or extracurricular activities (dance, yoga, sports teams, etc.). Finally, consider allowing the students to create their own tongue twisters or use tongue twisters they have heard in the past.

6. Say: *Now we are going to stretch our tongues and lips and warm up our ability to enunciate with a tongue twister or two. Repeat the words "unique New York" as many times and as quickly as you can without any mispronunciations. After approximately 20–30 seconds, say to students: Let's try a new one. Repeat the words "good gulp bad blood" as many times and as quickly as you can without any mispronunciations.* Let students work on this tongue twister for approximately 20–30 seconds.

- It is possible that some students may still be reluctant or bashful public speakers. While recognizing those students' reluctance, they should be encouraged and supported in preparing an oral presentation. Consider placing those students near other students who will encourage and support all classmates in speaking publicly as they engage in this activity.
- Some students might want to get too "silly" in their speeches. Rather than focusing on the criteria for the activity, they might focus on simply being funny or getting laughs. Remind students that while you want them to have fun you also expect them to take the activity seriously.

ACTIVITY: CREATE A SPEECH

Tell students that they will create a short epideictic, forensic, or political speech today. Given that the speeches will be short, students might create only a short excerpt from what would be a longer speech. Each speech should be 3 minutes or less. Also tell them that they will deliver their speech to the class during the next class.

7. Distribute Handout 9.1. Tell students that they will have 30 minutes to create an original speech of 2–3 minutes. Explain that each speech must be an epideictic, forensic, or political speech that reflects the use of ethos, logos, and/or pathos. Go over some options for the speeches (a eulogy, a campaign speech, a reduced homework or bring-a-pet-to-school policy in their school, etc.). Tell students that at least two appeals and one rhetorical device should be used in this speech. Tell students they will complete Handout 9.1 while developing their speeches to help ensure each of the criteria for this activity has been satisfied. Review Handout 9.1 with students to ensure comprehension of the task. Tell students that they will only have one class period to create, write, and practice their speeches. Reassure students that their speeches do not have to be "perfect" due to the limited amount of time allotted to the activity. Tell them that this activity is supposed to be a fun way to explore and demonstrate understanding of the concepts learned in the unit so far and to practice speaking alone in front of an audience.
8. Once students have completed Handout 9.1, they should draft a short speech in their Student Workbook.

Students should be able to go to areas in the classroom where they have room to practice their speeches. You may have to rearrange some desks/tables so students have room to create and practice out loud.

- The draft should be sufficiently developed so students can use it to practice their speeches out loud. Some students might wish to write the speech in a more final form and use the written speech to practice. However, students should be reminded that they will not read the speech.
- While students are practicing their speeches, quietly visit with each to ensure progress toward the activity goals. Provide guidance as necessary to ensure each student satisfies the criteria for the activity.

HOMEWORK

9. As a whole group, ask students whether they have any questions about the Create a Speech Activity and the speech they will deliver for the next lesson. Be sure all questions have been answered. Ask students to put their completed Handout 9.1 in their workbooks.
10. Ask students to spend time practicing their speeches out loud in front of a mirror for homework. Encourage them to let a friend or adult listen and offer feedback.

HANDOUT 9.1

CREATE A SPEECH CHECKLIST

Directions: Answer the following questions about your speech. Use a separate sheet of paper if necessary.

1. What type of speech will you create? Epideictic, forensic, or political?

2. Who is your audience?

3. What do you want your audience to do or believe?

4. What rhetorical appeals will you use? Why did you choose these appeals? Be specific.

HANDOUT 9.1, CONTINUED

5. How will you establish ethos? In other words, how will you establish goodwill and good moral character?

6. Describe the appropriate cadence, volume, and pitch you will use in your speech?

7. What rhetorical device(s) do you plan to use? Why did you choose these? Be specific.

8. Is your speech between 2 and 3 minutes?

9. Did you practice your speech out loud a few times?

LESSON 10 Perform Your Own Epideictic, Forensic, or Political Speech

MATERIALS

- ✓ Student journals
- ✓ Student workbooks
- ✓ Handout 2.2: Rhetoric Terminology: Rhetorical Devices
- ✓ Handout 9.1: Create a Speech Checklist (completed)
- ✓ Handout 10.1A: Formative Assessment 3 (hardest)
- ✓ Handout 10.1B: Formative Assessment 3 (on-level)
- ✓ Handout 10.1C: Formative Assessment 3 (easiest)
- ✓ Appendix B1: Grouping Plan Chart

- Rhetoric is an art that can be systematically studied.
- Rhetoricians use a variety of appeals to persuade an audience.
- Understanding the interests and values of an audience is key to persuasion.

OBJECTIVES

Students will:

- ✓ generate ideas for persuasive speaking,
- ✓ express ideas clearly and persuasively,
- ✓ use clear reasons and relevant evidence,
- ✓ identify the values and interests of an audience,
- ✓ use rhetorical appeals and devices in their own speaking, and
- ✓ use appropriate cadence, volume, and pitch when trying to persuade an audience.

- Ethos
- Pathos
- Logos
- Epideictic rhetoric
- Forensic rhetoric
- Political rhetoric

SEQUENCE

WARM UP

1. Say: *It's time for our daily journal reflection. But, this will be our last journal reflection as we will start to create individual rhetorical endeavors over the next few lessons. We have listened to several examples of excellent rhetoric including commercial and political advertisements, as well as epideictic, forensic, and political speeches. For today's journal activity, I'd like you to think about which of the rhetorical exemplars or videos we have heard so far that you found to be the least persuasive. Try to remember as many details as you can about the rhetorical exemplar that comes into your mind. What was unpersuasive about the speech or advertisement? What did you dislike about it? What rhetorical appeal(s) were not used effectively? Were there also ineffective rhetorical devices in the exemplar? What might you have done differently to make it more persuasive? I will give you 30 seconds to quietly get a clear memory of that rhetorical exemplar with lots of details in your mind.*

After the 30 seconds are up, ask students to describe in their journals (in writing or a drawing) which rhetorical exemplar each found to be the least persuasive. Remind students that they only have a couple of minutes to get down as many details as possible. When students have finished, ask them to turn and share their choices with their chair neighbor.

After pairs have shared, take a class poll to see which rhetorical exemplar was selected by the greatest number of students to be least persuasive. As a class, determine what was unappealing and unpersuasive about the exemplar.

ACTIVITY: VOCAL WARM UP

Remind students that, before giving a speech, good oral advocates need to exercise their voices and bodies to help them speak clearly. Invite students to stand up, close their eyes, and relax by taking deep breaths from their diaphragm (continue instructing students to breathe deeply until the room is quiet). Engage students in stretching for 2–3 minutes. For example, ask students to reach up to the ceiling as high as they can, and then slowly stretch down to their toes, to stretch from side to side with one arm over their head, to roll their shoulders and head around, etc.

2. Say: *Now we are going to stretch our tongues and lips and warm up our ability to enunciate with a tongue twister or two. Repeat the words "unique New York" as many times and as quickly as you can without any*

mispronunciations. After approximately 20–30 seconds, say: Let's try a new one. Repeat the words "good gulp bad blood" as many times and as quickly as you can without any mispronunciations. Let students work on this tongue twister for approximately 20–30 seconds.

ACTIVITY: PRESENT SPEECHES

Remind students that each student will have approximately 2–3 minutes to deliver his or her speech. Arrange a place in the classroom where students will have sufficient room to present speeches. Also make sure all audience members can see and hear the speeches.

- Place names in a "hat" and draw names to set the order of speeches.
- It might be necessary to remind students about class expectations for positive audience participation.

3. As each student comes to present, he or she should introduce the speech. The speaker should also identify the audience he or she intends to persuade to do or believe something. Students may refer to their completed Handout 9.1 for this.
4. After each speech, ask the class to identify what type of speech was delivered (epideictic, forensic, or political) which rhetorical appeals and devices were used. You can also ask for a brief discussion of what was effective about the speech or what changes could be suggested to make it more persuasive.
5. Ask students to put their completed Handout 9.1 in their workbooks.

PREPARATION: FORMATIVE ASSESSMENT 3

6. Administer Formative Assessment 3 before Lesson 11. As students' readiness levels may vary, Formative Assessment 3 is differentiated (Handouts 10.1A–C). A sorting chart is provided (Appendix B1):
   - ✓ **Group A:** Students have been able to identify consistently the rhetorical appeals and devices used in the rhetorical exemplars from Lessons 3–8. Students also used correctly rhetorical devices and appeals in their Lesson 10 speeches.
   - ✓ **Group B:** Students have been able to identify on most occasions the rhetorical appeals and devices used in the rhetorical exemplars from Lessons 3–8. Students also used correctly at least one rhetorical device and one rhetorical appeal in their Lesson 10 speeches, but they may have shown some confusion in their usage.
   - ✓ **Group C:** Students did not demonstrate the ability to identify the rhetorical appeals and devices used in the rhetorical exemplars from

Keep in mind that the three readiness groups are suggested or potential groups, but for a given class of students, not all might be applicable. For example, all of your students might fall into Groups B and C, or all might fall into Groups A and B, etc. In that case, you may not need to use all three versions of Formative Assessment 3.

Lessons 3–8 without support OR correctly use at least one rhetorical device and one rhetorical appeal in their Lesson 10 speeches without confusion. (You will work with Group C students on the assessment; see Handout 10.1C.)

PREPARATION: FOR NEXT LESSON

7. Read student responses to Formative Assessment 3 and make notes about students' understanding and progress at this point in the unit. Return Handout 10.1 to students and ask them to place it in their workbooks. If necessary, meet with students who are struggling with the concepts to date to clarify misunderstandings. It is essential that students are prepared at this point in the unit to create their rhetorical endeavor with a thorough understanding of the unit ideas and skills.

HANDOUT 10.1A

FORMATIVE ASSESSMENT 3

Directions: Below you will find an excerpt from John F. Kennedy's Inaugural Address from January 1961. Carefully read the excerpt. Using Handout 2.2: Rhetoric Terminology: Rhetorical Devices handout from Lesson 2, please identify the rhetorical devices you see in the speech on the next page. Then, in a short paragraph, describe whether or not you believe Kennedy used ethos, pathos, and logos, and whether it was used effectively.

PRESIDENT JOHN F. KENNEDY'S INAUGURAL ADDRESS, JANUARY 1961

We observe today not a victory of party but a celebration of freedom, symbolizing an end as well as a beginning, signifying renewal as well as change. For I have sworn before you and Almighty God the same solemn oath our forebears prescribed nearly a century and three-quarters ago.

The world is very different now. For man holds in his mortal hands the power to abolish all forms of human poverty and all forms of human life. And yet the same revolutionary beliefs for which our forebears fought are still at issue around the globe—the belief that the rights of man come not from the generosity of the state but from the hand of God.

We dare not forget today that we are the heirs of that first revolution. Let the word go forth from this time and place, to friend and foe alike, that the torch has been passed to a new generation of Americans—born in this century, tempered by war, disciplined by a hard and bitter peace, proud of our ancient heritage and unwilling to witness or permit the slow undoing of those human rights to which this nation has always been committed, and to which we are committed today at home and around the world.

Let every nation know, whether it wishes us well or ill, that we shall pay any price, bear any burden, meet any hardship, support any friend, oppose any foe to assure the survival and the success of liberty . . . .

My fellow citizens of the world, ask not what America will do for you, but what together we can do for the freedom of man.

Finally, whether you are citizens of America or citizens of the world, ask of us here the same high standards of strength and sacrifice which we ask of you. With a good conscience our only sure reward, with history the final judge of our deeds, let us go forth to lead the land we love, asking His blessing and His help, but knowing that here on earth God's work must truly be our own.

HANDOUT 10.1A, CONTINUED

RHETORICAL DEVICES

1. Rhetorical Device 1: ______________________
   Kennedy used this rhetorical device when he said:

2. Rhetorical Device 2: ______________________
   Kennedy used this rhetorical device when he said:

3. Rhetorical Device 3: ______________________
   Kennedy used this rhetorical device when he said:

4. Rhetorical Device 4: ______________________
   Kennedy used this rhetorical device when he said:

5. Rhetorical Device 5: ______________________
   Kennedy used this rhetorical device when he said:

HANDOUT 10.1A, CONTINUED

6. What type of speech was this (epideictic, forensic, or political)? ____________________

7. In a short paragraph, describe whether or not you believe Kennedy used ethos, pathos, and logos in his inaugural address, and whether it was used effectively.

HANDOUT 10.1B

FORMATIVE ASSESSMENT 3

Directions Below you will find an excerpt from John F. Kennedy's Inaugural Address from January 1961. Carefully read the excerpt. Using Handout 2.2: Rhetoric Terminology: Rhetorical Devices handout from Lesson 2, please identify the rhetorical devices you see in the speech on the next page. Then, in a short paragraph, describe whether or not you believe Kennedy used ethos, pathos, and logos, and whether it was used effectively.

PRESIDENT JOHN F. KENNEDY'S INAUGURAL ADDRESS, JANUARY 1961

We observe today **not a victory of party but a celebration of freedom**, symbolizing an end **as well as** a beginning, signifying renewal **as well as** change. For I have sworn before you and **Almighty God** the same solemn oath our **forebears** prescribed nearly a century and three-quarters ago.

The world is very different now. For man holds in his mortal hands the power to abolish all forms of human poverty and all forms of human life. And yet the same revolutionary beliefs for which our **forebears** fought are still at issue around the globe—**the belief that the rights of man come not from the generosity of the state but from the hand of God**.

We dare not forget today that we are the heirs of that first revolution. Let the word go **forth from** this time and place, to **friend and foe** alike, that the torch has been passed to a new generation of Americans—born in this century, tempered by war, disciplined by a hard and bitter peace, proud of our ancient **heritage** and unwilling to witness or permit the slow undoing of those human rights to which this **nation** has always been committed, and to which we are committed today at home and around the world.

Let every nation know, whether it wishes us well or ill, that we shall **pay any price, bear any burden, meet any hardship, support any friend, oppose any foe** to assure the survival and the success of **liberty** . . . .

My fellow citizens of the world, **ask not what America will do for you, but what together we can do for the freedom of man.**

Finally, whether you are citizens of America or citizens of the world, ask of us here the **same high standards of strength and sacrifice** which we ask of you. With a good conscience our only sure reward, with history the final judge of our deeds, let us go forth to **lead the land we love**, asking **His** blessing and **His** help, but knowing that here on earth **God's** work must truly be our own.

HANDOUT 10.1B, CONTINUED

RHETORICAL DEVICES

1. Rhetorical Device 1: ______________________
   Kennedy used this rhetorical device when he said:

2. Rhetorical Device 2: ______________________
   Kennedy used this rhetorical device when he said:

3. Rhetorical Device 3: ______________________
   Kennedy used this rhetorical device when he said:

4. Rhetorical Device 4: ______________________
   Kennedy used this rhetorical device when he said:

5. Rhetorical Device 5: ______________________
   Kennedy used this rhetorical device when he said:

HANDOUT 10.1B, CONTINUED

6. What type of speech was this (epideictic, forensic, or political)? ______________

7. In a short paragraph, describe whether or not you believe Kennedy used ethos, pathos, and logos in his inaugural address, and whether it was used effectively.

HANDOUT 10.1C

FORMATIVE ASSESSMENT 3

Directions: Together we are going to read an excerpt from John F. Kennedy's Inaugural Address from January 1961. We are going to look for rhetorical devices in this excerpt. Using your Handout 2.2: Rhetoric Terminology: Rhetorical Devices, together we will identify the rhetorical devices you see in the speech on the next page and match them to the correct text. The text that has been put in bold will give you clues. Then, you will independently describe whether or not you believe Kennedy used ethos, pathos, and logos, and whether it was used effectively.

PRESIDENT JOHN F. KENNEDY'S INAUGURAL ADDRESS, JANUARY 1961

We observe today **not a victory of party but a celebration of freedom**, symbolizing an end **as well as** a beginning, signifying renewal **as well as** change. For I have sworn before you and **Almighty God** the same solemn oath our **forebears** prescribed nearly a century and three-quarters ago.

The world is very different now. For man holds in his mortal hands the power to abolish all forms of human poverty and all forms of human life. And yet the same revolutionary beliefs for which our **forebears** fought are still at issue around the globe—**the belief that the rights of man come not from the generosity of the state but from the hand of God**.

We dare not forget today that we are the heirs of that first revolution. Let the word go **forth from** this time and place, to **friend and foe** alike, that the torch has been passed to a new generation of Americans—born in this century, tempered by war, disciplined by a hard and bitter peace, proud of our ancient **heritage** and unwilling to witness or permit the slow undoing of those human rights to which this **nation** has always been committed, and to which we are committed today at home and around the world.

Let every nation know, whether it wishes us well or ill, that we shall **pay any price, bear any burden, meet any hardship, support any friend, oppose any foe** to assure the survival and the success of **liberty** . . . .

My fellow citizens of the world, **ask not what America will do for you, but what together we can do for the freedom of man.**

Finally, whether you are citizens of America or citizens of the world, ask of us here the **same high standards of strength and sacrifice** which we ask of you. With a good conscience our only sure reward, with history the final judge of our deeds, let us go forth to **lead the land we love**, asking **His** blessing and **His** help, but knowing that here on earth **God's** work must truly be our own.

HANDOUT 10.1C, CONTINUED

RHETORICAL DEVICES

1. Rhetorical Device 1: ______________________________
   Kennedy used this rhetorical device when he said:

2. Rhetorical Device 2: ______________________________
   Kennedy used this rhetorical device when he said:

3. Rhetorical Device 3: ______________________________
   Kennedy used this rhetorical device when he said:

4. Rhetorical Device 4: ______________________________
   Kennedy used this rhetorical device when he said:

5. Rhetorical Device 5: ______________________________
   Kennedy used this rhetorical device when he said:

HANDOUT 10.1C, CONTINUED

6. What type of speech was this (epideictic, forensic, or political)? ______________________

7. In a short paragraph, describe whether or not you believe Kennedy used ethos, pathos, and logos in his inaugural address, and whether it was used effectively.

LESSON 11 Research Process Review (Optional)

Teacher's Note: This lesson is optional. Its purpose is to review the research process as students begin to conduct research in preparation for the Ode to Aristotle Rhetoric Gala.

MATERIALS

- ✓ Exploration and Communication (Unit 1) components including:
  - Handout 7.2: INSERT Poster
  - Appendix A2: Big6 Research Process Poster

Research is an organized and systematic way of finding answers to questions.

OBJECTIVES

Students will review:

- ✓ research strategies,
- ✓ note-taking strategies, and
- ✓ evaluation of texts

SEQUENCE

1. Review research strategies from Exploration and Communication: A Researcher's Journey (Unit 1).

This lesson assumes that teachers and students have completed Exploration and Communication: A Researcher's Journey. If not, teachers should review the research strategies that may be helpful and applicable to research for this unit.

This lesson may not be necessary for students who have successfully completed Exploration and Communication. For students who struggled with the unit, this optional lesson could be used to support their research for the Rhetoric Gala.

2. Ask students what they remember about the Big6 Research Strategies. Students should remember or be reminded that researchers work with a plan, and that they will need to develop a plan for researching the rhetorical endeavor that they will present at the Ode to Aristotle Rhetoric Gala.
3. Explain to students that once they have a general sense of their rhetorical endeavor speech topics, they will use the Big6 research steps to prepare their speech. For example, if students choose to create and deliver a eulogy on a historical figure of interest, they will need to conduct research on the life and accomplishments of the person eulogized. If they choose to create a forensic speech on an issue of interest, they will need to conduct research on their issue.

There may be "hot" issues that are being debated in the communities of students working on this unit. You might encourage students to consider a rhetorical endeavor on a local issue of interest.

4. Remind students that Step 1 in the Big6 Research Process is to answer the question: *What is the problem/task?* For their rhetorical endeavor, the students' task is to conduct research that will enable them to prepare a persuasive epideictic, forensic, or political speech, and to share findings with an audience in the form of a persuasive speech.
5. Remind students that Steps 2 and 4 in the research process are designed to engage in appropriate information-seeking strategies and to examine text features to better understand their resources. Students will need to determine what texts—usually nonfiction—will be most useful in preparation for their rhetorical endeavors. They may also need to be reminded of the text features that will help them identify the best information and resources.
6. Remind students that Step 3 in the research process is to determine how to locate and access appropriate resources for their research. You may have to work with the librarian or information technologist at your school to help students locate these resources.
7. Finally, remind students of the note-taking strategies from Step 5 that will support them in reducing the text into a form that is in their own words. This will be critical for both the speech writing and speech delivery components of the rhetorical endeavor.

PREPARATION: FOR NEXT LESSON

8. During the next lesson, students will begin to identify and select topics of the speeches they will write and deliver during the Ode to Aristotle Rhetoric Gala. If there is time for students to begin research, make sure that the technology and resources they will need for research is available.

LESSON

12 Rhetorical Endeavor Design

MATERIALS

- ✓ Student workbooks
- ✓ Handout 1.1: Unit Preassessment
- ✓ Handout 1.2A–C: Excerpts from Aristotle's *Rhetoric*
- ✓ Handouts 6.1A–C: Excerpts from Aristotle's *Rhetoric*, Book I: Chapter 3
- ✓ Handout 12.1: Summative Assessment Rubric
- ✓ Handout 12.2: Performance Assessment Rubric
- ✓ Handout 12.3: Rhetorical Endeavor Design Checklist

- Rhetoric is an art that can be studied systematically.
- Rhetoricians use a variety of appeals to persuade an audience to do or believe something.
- Understanding the interests and values of an audience is key to persuasion.

OBJECTIVES

Students will:

- ✓ generate ideas for persuasive speaking and oral advocacy, and
- ✓ participate as knowledgeable, reflective, and critical members of an engaged citizenry.

Students will need to retrieve Handouts 1.1, 1.2, and 6.2 from their workbooks so Aristotle's own words are available to discuss answers to these questions. In case there are a few students who have misplaced these handouts, have a few extra copies available.

SEQUENCE

WARM UP

1. Talk with students about the main big idea of this unit: *Rhetoric is an art that can be studied systematically*. Engage students in a discussion about what that big idea means to them at this point in the unit.

Pose these questions:

- How is rhetoric an art?
- Why did Aristotle say that it would be difficult for a speaker to persuade an audience if he or she did not establish ethos or good moral character?
- Why do you think Aristotle believed that logos was the best mode of persuasion?
- What is most effective in persuading you to do or believe something—ethos, pathos, or logos?
- Do you agree with Aristotle's contention that not only should a speaker be concerned with what he or she says, but how he or she says it? Why or why not?

Continue the discussion by saying: *For your final journal entries, we wrote about which of the rhetorical exemplars we listened to and watched that you believed was most, and then least, persuasive and effective. Let's talk one last time together about your responses and think about how you can apply the persuasive techniques to your own efforts to persuade, or avoid unpersuasive techniques.* Allow students the opportunity to wrap up with a discussion of these thoughts as they will provide strong synthesis of the big ideas of the unit as they begin to prepare their rhetorical endeavors.

INSTRUCTION: INTRODUCE RHETORICAL ENDEAVOR

Teachers should start thinking about extending invitations to family members, other students, and guests at this time. Consider inviting local advertisers, lawyers, politicians, or others who are engaged in "persuading" professions. Solicit ideas about desired guests from your students as well.

2. Tell students that today they have a very big decision to make. They must decide what type of rhetorical endeavor they will undertake and perform at the Ode to Aristotle Rhetoric Gala, as well as the topic of the rhetorical endeavor. Let students know that within a matter of days (you can be more exact when you've set the gala date), they will present their rhetorical endeavor speeches to a real audience. This audience will be made up of students and different adults in their community. These speeches will be a final assessment for the unit.
3. Distribute Handouts 12.1 and 12.2. Explain that each student will independently create a speech to perform at the Ode to Aristotle Rhetoric Gala. More specifically, each student will create an epideictic, political, or forensic speech lasting between 4 and 6 minutes. Inform students that they cannot read their speech but must present it using only abbreviated notes. As an additional assessment for the unit, students will also be asked to evaluate a speech given by a classmate. This is the performance assessment. Let students know that the rubric you will use to assess them is the same rubric they will use to peer assess.
4. Instruct students that they can be creative in their speeches. For example, if they chose to create an epideictic eulogy of a famous or historic person, they can pretend to be that person's spouse, friend, child, etc. to boost their ethos. As another creative example, students who wish to deliver a political (deliberative) speech on a policy or topic of interest can pretend that they are an expert or a lawyer or a politician with expertise on the topic.

Ask students to review Handouts 12.1 and 12.2. Carefully read through the rubrics with students and discuss expectations for their speeches. Give students time to review the rubrics and to ask questions about the rhetorical endeavor assignment.

INSTRUCTION: RESEARCH ENDEAVOR

5. Discuss the type of research that will be necessary for each type of speech.

If a student chooses to perform a eulogy on a historic figure, biographies and autobiographies would be appropriate resources for research. A campaign speech might require Internet research to determine what issues are important to voters. (If you chose to implement Lesson 11, much of this information would have been addressed.)

6. Distribute Handout 12.3. Explain to students that they will complete the checklist, which is designed to be an additional aid to help them think through and plan their rhetorical endeavors. Ask students to read through Handout 12.3. When they have finished, ask if they have any questions about designing their rhetorical endeavor and completing the checklist.

As students begin to design their rhetorical endeavors, allow students to brainstorm ideas with a partner or the student they sit next to if they are struggling to develop ideas for their rhetorical endeavor.

- When you have answered all student questions, students should begin to complete Handout 12.3. You should make yourself available to students as they brainstorm the design of their rhetorical endeavors.
- Students will not be able to complete Handout 12.3 before they complete their research, but they should get started on as much as they can at this phase.

HOMEWORK

7. Again ask students if they have any questions about how to design their rhetorical endeavor. Ask students to complete as much of Handout 12.3 as they can for homework.

HANDOUT 12.1

SUMMATIVE ASSESSMENT RUBRIC

Speaker's Name: ______________________________

Subject Of speech: ______________________________

Category	Master	Journeyman	Apprentice	Teacher Comments
Use of Appeals	Student used ethos, pathos, and logos effectively and throughout the speech.	Student used ethos, pathos, or logos somewhat effectively during some of the speech.	Student did not use ethos, pathos, and logos effectively throughout the speech.	
Rhetorical Devices	Student used at least three rhetorical devices effectively during speech.	Student used one or two rhetorical devices effectively during speech.	Student did not use rhetorical devices effectively during speech.	
Audience	Student clearly understood the values and interests of the audience throughout the speech.	Student understood the values and interests of the audience during some of the speech.	Student did not understand the values and interests of the audience during most or all of the speech.	
Cadence, Volume, Pitch	Student used the appropriate cadence, volume, and pitch throughout the speech.	Student used the appropriate cadence, volume, and pitch during some parts of the speech.	Student did not used the appropriate cadence, volume, and pitch during most or any of the speech.	
Preparedness	Student delivered the presentation without reading from the written speech, using only notes to help student stay on track.	Student read only a few portions of the written speech during the presentation.	Student relied excessively on the written speech during the presentation.	
Overall Persuasiveness	Student demonstrated strong knowledge of the topic of his/her speech and used clear reasons and relevant evidence in order to persuade the audience.	Student demonstrated some knowledge of the topic of his/her speech or used some reasons and relevant evidence in order to persuade the audience.	Student did not demonstrate strong knowledge of the topic of his/her speech or use clear reasons and relevant evidence in order to persuade the audience.	
Points	**Mastery:** ________	**Journeyman:** ________	**Apprentice:** ________	**Total Points:** ________

HANDOUT 12.2

PERFORMANCE ASSESSMENT RUBRIC

Speaker's Name: ______________________________

Title of speech: ______________________________

Category	Master	Journeyman	Apprentice	Student Comments
Use of Appeals	Student used ethos, pathos, and logos effectively and throughout the speech.	Student used ethos, pathos, or logos somewhat effectively during some of the speech.	Student did not use ethos, pathos, and logos effectively throughout the speech.	
Rhetorical Devices	Student used at least three rhetorical devices effectively during speech.	Student used one or two rhetorical devices effectively during speech.	Student did not use rhetorical devices effectively during speech.	
Audience	Student clearly understood the values and interests of the audience throughout the speech.	Student understood the values and interests of the audience during some of the speech.	Student did not understand the values and interests of the audience during most or all of the speech.	
Cadence, Volume, Pitch	Student used the appropriate cadence, volume, and pitch throughout the speech.	Student used the appropriate cadence, volume, and pitch during some parts of the speech.	Student did not used the appropriate cadence, volume, and pitch during most or any of the speech.	
Preparedness	Student delivered the presentation without reading from the written speech, using only notes to help student stay on track.	Student read only a few portions of the written speech during the presentation.	Student relied excessively on the written speech during the presentation.	
Overall Persuasiveness	Student demonstrated strong knowledge of the topic of his/her speech and used clear reasons and relevant evidence in order to persuade the audience.	Student demonstrated some knowledge of the topic of his/her speech or used some reasons and relevant evidence in order to persuade the audience.	Student did not demonstrate strong knowledge of the topic of his/her speech or use clear reasons and relevant evidence in order to persuade the audience.	
Points	**Mastery:** ________	**Journeyman:** ________	**Apprentice:** ________	**Total Points:** ________

In the space below or on the back of this sheet, please provide additional constructive feedback regarding your classmate's rhetorical endeavor.

HANDOUT 12.3

RHETORICAL ENDEAVOR DESIGN CHECKLIST

______ I know what type of rhetorical endeavor I will create (check one).

- ❑ Epideictic
- ❑ Forensic
- ❑ Political

______ I know who my audience will be. The members of my audience are:

______ I know what I want my audience to do or believe. I want to persuade my audience to:

______ I know what type of research and resources will be necessary for me to prepare my Rhetorical Endeavor. The resources I need are:

______ I will establish and use ethos in my speech. I will establish and use ethos by:

______ I will establish and use logos in my speech. I will establish and use logos by:

HANDOUT 12.3, CONTINUED

______ I will establish and use pathos in my speech. I will establish and use pathos by:

______ I will use at least three rhetorical devices in my speech. The three rhetorical devices I will use are:

1. ______________________________

2. ______________________________

3. ______________________________

______ My speech will be between 4 and 6 minutes. I will time my speech to make sure it is between 4 and 6 minutes.

My use of rhetorical appeals will make my speech more effective because:

The rhetorical devices I chose will make my speech more effective because

LESSON

13 Rhetorical Endeavor Research

Teacher's Note: During this lesson, which will likely take more than one day, you will support students as they conduct research for the Ode to Aristotle Rhetoric Gala.

MATERIALS

- ✓ Student workbooks
- ✓ Handout 12.1: Summative Assessment Rubric
- ✓ Handout 12.2: Performance Assessment Rubric
- ✓ Handout 12.3: Rhetorical Endeavor Design Checklist

- Rhetoric is an art that can be studied systematically.
- Rhetoricians use a variety of appeals to persuade an audience to do or believe something.
- Understanding the interests and values of an audience is key to persuasion.

OBJECTIVES

Students will:

- ✓ participate as knowledgeable, reflective, creative, and critical members of a rhetorical community;
- ✓ identify the values and interests of an audience; and
- ✓ use clear reasons and relevant evidence in their writing to persuade.

SEQUENCE

ACTIVITY: INDEPENDENT RESEARCH SESSION

Tell students that today they will conduct research for the rhetorical endeavor they will present at the ode to Aristotle Rhetoric Gala. This lesson may take a few days as students should have plenty of time to research their speeches. Be sure to have materials from the Exploration and Communication unit available (e.g., Big6 Research Strategies) for students to consult for appropriate research strategies.

1. You may want to station the librarian in the library while you work in the classroom. This way, students who require additional research time can go to the library while students who are already synthesizing information into their presentation can remain in the classroom.
2. Remind students to consistently consult the rubric (Handout 12.1) to make sure they are on track to produce high quality work. They should also use Handout 12.3 as a checklist of expectations for the rhetorical endeavor.
3. Leave some time at the end of Lesson 13 to answer final research questions before students begin to write their rhetorical endeavors.

LESSON

14 Rhetorical Endeavor Writing

Teacher's Note: For this lesson, which may take more than one day, you will continue to support students as they prepare for the Ode to Aristotle Rhetoric Gala.

MATERIALS

- ✓ Student workbooks
- ✓ Handout 1.1: Unit Preassessment
- ✓ Handout 12.1: Summative Assessment Rubric
- ✓ Handout 12.2: Performance Assessment Rubric
- ✓ Handout 12.3: Rhetorical Endeavor Design Checklist

- Rhetoric is an art that can be studied systematically.
- Rhetoric serves as a call to action.
- Rhetoricians use a variety of appeals to persuade an audience to do or believe something.
- Understanding the interests and values of an audience is key to persuasion.

OBJECTIVES

Students will:

- ✓ generate ideas for persuasive speaking and oral advocacy,
- ✓ use clear reasons and relevant evidence in their writing to persuade,
- ✓ express idea clearly and persuasively,
- ✓ use rhetorical appeals in their own writing,
- ✓ use rhetorical devices in their own writing, and
- ✓ participate as knowledgeable, reflective, and critical members of an engaged citizenry.

SEQUENCE

ACTIVITY: INDEPENDENT WRITING SESSION

1. As students complete their rhetorical endeavor research, it is time for them to write the speeches they will deliver at the Ode to Aristotle Rhetoric Gala. Explain to students that the purpose for writing the speech is to organize their thinking and to ensure that they have met the requirements of the assignment. However, they will not be able to read the written speech at the gala. Rather, they will be expected to deliver their speech with only a few notes to keep them on track. Reassure them that they will have plenty of time to practice before the gala.
2. Remind students to consistently consult Handouts 12.1 and 12.2 (the rubrics) to make sure they are on track to produce high-quality work. They should also refer to Handout 12.3 (the Rhetorical Endeavor Design Checklist) to further help keep them on track.
3. Remind students that their speech should take between 4 and 6 minutes to deliver. Tell them that after they write their speeches they will practice speeches out loud several times to make sure they have enough (or not too much) material to allow 4–6 minutes of speaking.
4. As students turn their research into speeches, monitor student progress. It would be a good idea to hold individual student conferences to check on student progress and offer feedback to support all students in meeting the goals of the summative assessment.

LESSON

15 Practice for Ode to Aristotle Rhetoric Gala

MATERIALS

- ✓ Student journals
- ✓ Student workbooks
- ✓ Stopwatches or clocks for timing rhetorical endeavors
- ✓ Mirrors if available
- ✓ Index cards
- ✓ Handout 12.1: Summative Assessment Rubric
- ✓ Handout 12.2: Performance Assessment Rubric (copies for students for practice peer assessing)

- Rhetoric is an art that can be systematically studied.
- Rhetoricians use a variety of appeals to persuade an audience.
- Understanding the interests and values of an audience is key to persuasion.

OBJECTIVES

Students will:

- ✓ express ideas clearly and persuasively;
- ✓ use clear reasons and relevant evidence;
- ✓ identify the values and interests of an audience;
- ✓ use rhetorical appeals and devices in their own speaking;
- ✓ use appropriate cadence, volume, and pitch when trying to persuade an audience; and
- ✓ participate as knowledgeable, reflective, and critical members of an engaged citizenry.

SEQUENCE

WARM UP

Remind students that, before giving a speech, good oral advocates need to exercise their voices and bodies to help them speak clearly. Because they will be practicing their rhetorical endeavors, it is essential that their voices are warmed up. Invite students to stand up, close their eyes, and relax by taking deep breaths from their diaphragm (continue instructing students to breathe deeply until the room is quiet). Engage students in stretching for 2–3 minutes. For example, ask students to reach up to the ceiling as high as they can, and then slowly stretch down to their toes, to stretch from side to side with one arm over their head, to roll their shoulders and head around, etc.

To vary this activity, consider allowing a student or group of students to lead the class in this vocal warm-up exercise. Also, consider allowing students to use different stretching activities that they may have used in physical education classes or extracurricular activities (dance, yoga, sports teams, etc.). Finally, consider allowing the students to create their own tongue twisters or use tongue twisters they have heard in the past.

1. Say: *Now we are going to stretch our tongues and lips and warm up our ability to enunciate with a tongue twister or two. Repeat the words "unique New York" as many times and as quickly as you can without any mispronunciations.* After approximately 20–30 seconds, say: *Let's try a new one. Repeat the words "good gulp bad blood" as many times and as quickly as you can without any mispronunciations.* Let students work on this tongue twister for approximately 20–30 seconds.

ACTIVITY: PRACTICE RHETORICAL ENDEAVORS

2. Remind students that each will have between 4 and 6 minutes to present a rhetorical endeavor at the Ode to Aristotle Rhetoric Gala. To ensure that the presentations fall within that time frame, students need to practice out loud and time themselves while delivering the speech. Remind students that they will not be allowed to read their speeches and that expert rhetoricians, including politicians and lawyers, always practice their speeches before delivering them. Engage students in a discussion of why it is important to be able to deliver a speech without reading, and how that will help build their ethos.

Make sure students are dispersed throughout the classroom so that they can hear themselves as they practice. At first, students should practice using the written speech. This will help them stay organized and on point while practicing.

Remind students to pay attention to their cadence, volume, and pitch. If there are mirrors available to the students, ask students to take turns practicing their speeches out loud in front of the mirror. This will help students pay attention to behaviors that might detract from the speech such as playing with hair, slouching, etc.

3. After students have practiced with the written speech three or four times, or until they are comfortable, they should start to use only notes. The index cards on which students wrote their research could serve as organizing notes or cue cards for this activity. Alternatively, students might need to create index cards with only bulleted notes to keep them

on track while speaking. Ultimately students should be able to deliver their speech without reading.

4. Ask students to get in pairs or small groups of three to four with students they don't usually work with. Tell students to take turns presenting their rhetorical endeavors without reading from the written speech.

Ask partner(s) to provide feedback using Handout 12.2: Performance Assessment Rubric. Make sure that partners can identify the use of ethos, pathos, and logos, and the rhetorical devices of their partner(s), as well as feedback on their partners' cadence, pitch, and volume or nonverbal ticks the peer engages in. Rotate so students have the opportunity practice and time their entire speech out loud at least two to three times.

PREPARATION: FOR NEXT LESSON

5. Remind students to invite parents, guardians, and guests to the Ode to Aristotle Rhetoric Gala. Discuss proper behavior for an audience during the gala. If you have any expectations for attire during the gala, discuss these expectations.
6. Require that students continue to practice their rhetorical endeavors in front of mirror out loud at home. Suggest that students also practice in front of parent or sibling or friend.
7. Decide the order in which students will present their rhetorical endeavors. Determine who each student will peer evaluate. You can assign pairs, assign based on similar interests or speech types, randomly, or any way that you deem appropriate. Make sure you have everything necessary to set up for the gala. Sufficient space and chairs should be available for guests.

LESSON 16 Ode to Aristotle Rhetoric Gala

MATERIALS

- ✓ Handout 12.1: Summative Assessment Rubric (teacher copies)
- ✓ Handout 12.2: Performance Assessment Rubric

- Rhetoric is an art that can be systematically studied.
- Rhetoricians use a variety of appeals to persuade an audience.
- Understanding the interests and values of an audience is key to persuasion.

OBJECTIVES

Students will:

- ✓ express ideas clearly and persuasively;
- ✓ use clear reasons and relevant evidence;
- ✓ identify the values and interests of an audience;
- ✓ use rhetorical appeals and devices in their own speaking;
- ✓ use appropriate cadence, volume, and pitch when trying to persuade an audience; and
- ✓ participate as knowledgeable, reflective, and critical members of an engaged citizenry.

SEQUENCE

1. Make sure you have set up for the Ode to Aristotle Rhetoric Gala. Welcome guests. Explain what the students have learned during the course of the unit. You might ask students to briefly explain the highlights of their own learning.

Be ready with your order for student presentations. Also, let students know who they will peer evaluate and ask them to write the name of that student on Handout 12.2.

2. **Summative assessment:** Call up students one by one to present. Assess students using the Summative Assessment Rubric (Handout 12.1). You should provide comments on the rubric for each student to inform them of their progress.
3. **Performance assessment:** Distribute Handout 12.2. Explain that they will evaluate a peer's rhetorical endeavor as a way to provide feedback to the peer and as an additional way for you to monitor their progress.

References

Burns, D. E. (1987). *The effects of group training activities on students' creative productivity* (Unpublished doctoral dissertation). University of Connecticut, Storrs.

Callahan, C. M., Moon, T. R., Oh, S., Azano, A. & Hailey, E. (2015). Documenting the effects of an integrated curricular/instructional model for gifted students. *American Educational Research Journal, 52,* 137–167.

Csikszentmihalyi, M. (1990). *Flow: The psychology of optimal experience.* New York, NY: Harper & Row.

Csikszentmihalyi, M., Rathunde, K. R., & Whalen, S. (1993). *Talented teenagers: The roots of success and failure.* New York, NY: Cambridge University Press.

Donovan, M., Bransford, J., & Pellegrino, J. (1999). *How people learn: Bridging research and practice.* Washington, DC: National Academy Press.

Eisenberg, M., & Berkowitz, R. (1987). *The Big6.* Retrieved from http://big6.com

Freire, P. (1970). *Pedagogy of the oppressed* (M. B. Ramos, Trans.). New York, NY: Continuum.

Freire, P., & Macedo, D. (1987). *Literacy: Reading the word and the world.* Westport, CT: Bergin & Garvey.

Howard, P. (1994). *An owner's manual for the brain.* Austin, TX: Leorian Press.

Jensen, E. (1998). *Teaching with the brain in mind.* Alexandria, VA: Association for Supervision & Curriculum Development.

Kaplan, S. (2013). Depth and complexity. In C. M. Callahan & H. L. Hertberg-Davis (Eds.), *Fundamentals of gifted education* (pp. 277–287). New York, NY: Routledge.

Kaplan, S. (2005). Layering differential curricula for gifted and talented. In F. A. Karnes & S. M. Bean (Eds.), *Methods and materials for teaching gifted students* (2nd ed., pp. 107–132). Waco, TX: Prufrock Press.

National Association for Gifted Children. (2010). *Pre-K to Grade 12 Gifted Programming Standards.* Retrieved from http://www.nagc.org/index.aspx?id=546

National Council of Teachers of English, & International Reading Association. (2012). *Standards for the English language arts.* Urbana, IL: NCTE.

Olenchak, F. R. (1991). Assessing program effects for gifted/learning disabled students. In R. Swassing & A. Robinson (Eds.), *NAGC 1991 research briefs* (pp. 86–89). Washington, DC: National Association for Gifted Children.

Reis, S. M. (1981). *An analysis of the productivity of gifted students participating in programs using the Revolving Door Identification Model* (Unpublished doctoral dissertation). University of Connecticut, Storrs.

Renzulli, J. S. (1977). *The enrichment triad model: A guide for developing defensible programs for the gifted and talented.* Mansfield Center, CT: Creative Learning Press.

Renzulli, J. S., & Reis, S. (1985). *The schoolwide enrichment model: A comprehensive plan for educational excellence.* Mansfield Center, CT: Creative Learning Press.

Renzulli, J. S., & Reis, S. (2001). The schoolwide enrichment model. In K. Heller, F. Mönks, R. Sternberg, & R. Subotnik (Eds.), *International handbook of giftedness and talent* (2nd ed., pp. 367–382). Oxford, England: Elsevier Science.

Saylor, R. N., & Shadel, M. (2011). *Tongue-tied America: Reviving the art of verbal persuasion.* New York, NY: Aspen.

Schack, G. D., Starko, A. J., & Burns, D. E. (1991). Self-efficacy and creative productivity: Three studies of above average ability children. *Journal of Research in Education, 1,* 44–52.

Sousa, D., & Tomlinson, C. (2010). *Differentiation and the brain: How neuroscience supports the learner-friendly classroom.* Bloomington, IN: Solution Tree.

Tomlinson, C. A. (1995). *How to differentiate instruction in mixed-ability classrooms.* Alexandria, VA: Association for Supervision and Curriculum Development.

Tomlinson, C. A. (1999). *The differentiated classroom: Responding to the needs of all learners.* Alexandria, VA: Association for Supervision and Curriculum Development.

Wenglinsky, H. (2002). How schools matter: The link between teacher classroom practices and student academic performance. *Education Policy Analysis Archives, 10*(12). Retrieved from http://epaa.asu.edu/ojs/article/view/291

Appendices

Unit Resources

APPENDIX A1

BIG6 INSTRUCTIONS

BECOME AN EXPLORER

TASK DEFINITION		**Step 1: Task Definition** Students are told what they are required to do. In this unit, students will be investigating a question or topic of interest and exploring various nonfiction texts to find an answer to that question or gain a deep understanding of the topic. For the final product, students can choose one of three forms to showcase their learning—a paper, presentation, or performance. Both you and the students should be very clear on the requirements for the project (see Handout 12.2: Research Gala Rubric).
INFORMATION SEEKING STRATEGIES		**Step 2: Information Seeking Strategies** Students brainstorm the information they need in order to fully investigate the question/topic. This will require the teacher to highlight all of the possible nonfiction sources students could consult. Some of these sources include but are not limited to: newspapers, magazines, encyclopedias, books, and various online sources. Students should be encouraged to consider alternate sources to the school library. Perhaps a personal interview would be a perfect source for certain explorations! You want to get the students to think like real explorers/researchers!
LOCATION AND ACCESS		**Step 3: Location and Access** Actually finding sources is more difficult than you think. Even harder is sifting through a book to find relevant information. You will help students through this process. Enlist the help of the librarian for this entire unit.
USE OF INFORMATION		**Step 4: Use of Information** Students will determine the best methods to record the information they find. Will they take notes on paper? Note cards? Computer? Students will have to learn (on an elementary level) how to give credit to the sources they use. For this part of the unit, students will be given a researcher's notebook and taught a particular note-taking strategy.
SYNTHESIS		**Step 5: Synthesis** Students will work to carefully combine all of their findings into a coherent final product. Students will need instruction, time, and support to do this. Final product choices include: paper, presentation, or performance.
EVALUATION		**Step 6: Evaluation** Students will have their work evaluated, as well as evaluate the work of others. Students should be on track during the entire process because they have been working with the Research Gala Rubric and know exactly what they need to do.

Note. Adapted from *Big6*™ by Michael B. Eisenberg and Robert E. Berkowitz, 1987, retrieved from: http://www.big6.com. Copyright Michael B. Eisenberg and Robert E. Berkowitz, 1987. Adapted with permission.

APPENDIX A2

BIG6 RESEARCH PROCESS POSTER

BIG6
RESEARCH PROCESS

1 TASK DEFINITION

- What is the problem/task?
- What information do I need to solve the problem?
- How will I present my findings? (Format)

2 INFORMATION SEEKING STRATEGIES

- What sources do I need for this task?
- How will I determine quality sources?

3 LOCATION AND ACCESS

- Where can I find needed sources?
- How can I find relevant information within the sources?

4 USE OF INFORMATION

- How do I extract pertinent information from a source?
- How will I record important information?

5 SYNTHESIS

- How do I put all of the information together?
- How will I present my findings?

6 EVALUATION

- Did I complete the required task?
- How will I judge the quality of my work?

Note. Adapted from *Big6*™ by Michael B. Eisenberg and Robert E. Berkowitz, 1987, retrieved from: http://www.big6.com. Copyright Michael B. Eisenberg and Robert E. Berkowitz, 1987. Adapted with permission.

APPENDIX A3

CHOOSING GOOD RESEARCH QUESTIONS ANSWER KEY

☒ 1. Who invented the pencil?
A who question is too easy to answer. Instead, a student may want to find out how pencils came into use, how pencils are mass produced, or some specific question about how writing implements have changed over time.

☑ 2. Why do many people want to eat organic food?
To be more specific, a student may ask what are the major differences between conventional and organic foods and tie those to health.

☑ 3. How does the iPod work?
This is a good question that might be beefed up even more with a bit of history as to how it was developed and what changes have been implemented.

☒ 4. What are all of the holidays celebrated around the world?
This is way too broad. A student could choose to compare a holiday that is similar around the world, such as Independence Day celebrations.

☒ 5. Who came up with the idea for cell phones?
Because the questions asks "who," it is way too narrow. Instead, specific questions about how cell phones work or how they were developed would offer broader views.

☒ 6. Which sport is the best?
This is too broad. A more specific question related to a specific benefit, such as "What sports are best for cardiovascular fitness?" If something like this is chosen, an explanation of the benefit should be included.

☒ 7. When is the best time to get a new pet?
This could be improved with a more specific target, such as what are important qualities that pet owners need to have, or looking at specific pets and what sort of care they need.

☑ 8. Why do students have to take state tests in school?
A history of how government mandated state testing might prove interesting to students.

☑ 9. How can we help endangered species?
More specifically, how have scientists been able to improve the chances for survival for endangered species and/or how do organizations help endangered species.

APPENDIX A3, CONTINUED

☒ 10. Who won the Superbowl last year?
There's just one answer here. A more interesting question might look at the history of the Superbowl, how it got started, or major changes that have occurred.

APPENDIX A4
SAMPLE THINK-ALOUD

Directions: Use this think aloud to strengthen students' understanding of questions suitable for research:

It looks like we can't agree on whether this question would be a good research question or not: *How many kinds of dinosaurs were there?* I'm going to do some thinking about this question. First I'm going to ask myself about the topic, the main idea of the question.

First of all, I don't think I'd pick this topic for my research project unless I was very interested in it, so I'll ask myself if I would want to spend a few weeks trying to answer this question. I'm pretty interested in dinosaurs, so this might be a good question for me to research.

Next, I'd want to know if there was going to be any information on my topic. Well, I *know* there are lots of books and Internet resources on dinosaurs. I wonder if there is *enough* information on my topic. Based on how many things about dinosaurs I have read, I'd say there is enough information on the topic that I would be able to do my research. If I'm not sure, what would I do? (Elicit student answers.)

Hmm . . . now I'm wondering if there is *so much* information on my topic that I'll never be able to get finished with my project. No, because I'm not trying to find out everything about every kind of dinosaur, I just want to know how many kinds there were.

So far, I think my research topic is pretty good: I'm interested in it, I think I can find information about it, and I don't think it's too big of a topic or too small of one.

Next I should think about the way I would answer this question. Since I'm learning how to do a research project, I want a question that I can really research well, one that I can spend time on and do a really good job on.

I know that research takes time. You can't just find your answer in one hour. Would it take me a lot of time to find the answer to this question? Probably it would.

Now, is this the kind of question that would require me to look at a lot of resources to find my answer? Gosh, I don't know. There could be a book that tells exactly how many different kinds of dinosaurs there were. If there was a book like that, then I'd have my answer without doing research at all. I'd find the right answer in that book.

What if people couldn't agree on the right answer, though? What if people disagreed about the types of dinosaurs? What if one scientist said, "Well, this dinosaur and that dinosaur are in the same family," but somebody else said, "No, they're not." That second scientist might say there was a different number.

APPENDIX A4, CONTINUED

I'm going to look back at my question again: *How many kinds of dinosaurs were there?* I might find a different answer depending on whose books I read and whose point of view I agree with. But I wouldn't even know whose viewpoint was best unless I found out about the difference between the scientists' ways of categorizing dinosaurs. The question I would *really* be researching would be, *How do scientists categorize dinosaurs?*

I think that's a better research question than the first one, because it couldn't possibly have just one easy answer. If I researched that question, I'd find out a lot about all kinds of dinosaurs and about how scientists study them. That sounds really interesting to me.

APPENDIX A5

QUESTION FLOWCHART

TOPIC

Part 1: What words are associated with my topic?

Part 2: What questions can I generate about my topic using these associated words?

Types of questions: Put questions into the chart according to how they were written by students.

WHO	WHAT	WHEN	WHERE	WHY	HOW	WHICH

OPTIONAL MINI-LESSON ON THICK/THIN QUESTIONS

Complete chart activity (see instructions below).

Use checklist for "A good research question . . . "

Discuss which types of questions are most likely to be good research questions.

RESEARCH QUESTION

APPENDIX A5, CONTINUED

TOPIC

Part 1: What words are associated with my topic?
Ocean, krill, blubber, mammal, blue whale, endangered . . .

Part 2: What questions can I generate about my topic using these associated words?

Types of questions: Put questions into the chart according to how they were written by students.

WHO	WHAT	WHEN	WHERE	WHY	HOW	WHICH	OTHER
Who is the main scientist studying whales? *Who eats whale meat?*	*What kinds of whales are there?* *What do whales eat?*	*When were whales discovered?* *When did the Japanese start hunting whales?*	*Where do blue whales live?* *Where are whales most endangered?*	*Why don't whales lay eggs like fish?* *Why do people hunt whales?*	*How many kinds of whales are there?* *How do whales stay underwater for so long?*	*Which whales taste the best?* *Which ocean has the most whales?* *Which kind of whale is the smallest?*	*(See* **Tips** *below.)*

OPTIONAL MINI-LESSON ON THICK/THIN QUESTIONS

Tips: Make another category for questions that don't fit these categories (e.g., Do whales sleep? Is a whale a mammal?). Example: The underlined question above (How many . . .) should be moved to the other category because it's not like other "how" questions. Explain that "how many" is a question about quantity, not a question about process.

RESEARCH QUESTION

APPENDIX A6

ANECDOTAL RECORD FORM

Student	Date	Conference Contents
		Goal:
		Goal:
		Goal:

APPENDIX A7

TEACHER SCRIPT FOR MOCK PRESENTATION/EVALUATION SESSION

Below are two scripts for demonstrating what to do and what not to do while presenting research. These scripts are guides, meaning that it is not necessary for you to follow it exactly. The important thing is to effectively demonstrate for your students what makes a good presentation!

WHAT NOT TO DO

For this scenario, you are to be a terrible presenter. You can achieve this by inserting a lot of stalling words into your speech ("ummm," "you know," "like"), reading directly from your paper and avoiding eye contact, and fidgeting.

Okay, ummm . . . (giggle nervously). I'm not really sure what to say. Ummm . . . yeah. So, I researched dogs? Because I like dogs.

So, I wanted to know more about dogs. I looked on one website and found everything I needed to know.

All right, let's see. Well, you take the puppy to the vet to get it medicine. Wait! First you should research what kind of dog you want. It's important to get a dog that will fit in well with your family. It can be from the SPCA or a breeder. And you also need to buy things to have ready before getting the puppy.

Make sure you've puppy proofed your house. Keep things relaxed for your puppy for the first week. And have fun!

I think I may have forgotten some stuff, but that's about it.

WHAT TO DO

Practice this script so that you can smoothly present it to your students. Speak in a clear voice and make eye contact.

What does a person need to do in order to care for a puppy? That is what I wanted to investigate for my research project. I first started with a broad interest about dogs, but decided to focus on puppy care. By reading many different books and websites, I discovered that there is a lot of information to be learned about puppy care. If you're thinking about getting a puppy, you should do research on your own to prepare. Today I will share with you a few important puppy care tips.

Tip 1: Make sure your house is ready for a puppy. Put away toys, wires, and anything else a puppy might chew to pieces.

Tip 2: Work on housebreaking your puppy right away.

Tip 3: Feed your puppy the right diet (that means no human food!).

APPENDIX A7, CONTINUED

Tip 4: Take your puppy to the vet. The vet will give your puppy important medicine and vaccinations, as well as be able to provide you with advice.

Tip 5: Provide exercise and play time for your puppy. Both are important!

Tip 6: Go to school! Puppies need to learn polite manners as well, and obedience school is a fun place for them to do so.

Like I said, these are just a few tips about how to care for a puppy. It can be a fun challenge, and one that calls for a lot of responsibility. Make sure to be prepared, and both you and your puppy can enjoy a happy life together.

APPENDIX A8

SAMPLE LETTER

Dear Dr. Dugan,

Thank you for contacting me about your current research investigation. Due to extensive research I have recently conducted, I feel that I can provide you with a feasible and effective research design.

First, you want to make sure you and anyone who is working with you have a clear understanding of the research question and the final product. It seems to me that your task is to determine the top 100 most influential Americans and your final product is a book. Before you dig into the research, consider determining what you and your assistants already know about the most influential Americans. Are there any people that you all agree should be on the list even before you begin to research?

Second, you will want to determine what sources you will use to help you answer your research question: Who are the most influential Americans of all time? It seems to me, considering your current topic, magazines and newspapers will be better sources for you than encyclopedias and books.

Third, you will want to locate and access these sources. Finding the source can be easy, but finding the relevant information within the sources can be hard. A couple of things to be aware of: (1) Finding resources on the Internet is tricky because people can say anything they want on there. Check to see if you can find who writes, updates, or publishes the website and check their credentials. (2) Check the publication dates of any source you use, you don't want to use something too old and outdated.

Fourth, you will want to read texts and organize your notes so you can easily refer to them later. You may want to try a note-taking system with only one piece of information on each card. Also, make sure each notecard is tied to a source; this will make creating citations easier.

Fifth, you will want to synthesize your notes/findings. You will need to determine the best way to share your findings with your intended audience. From your letter, it seems that you have already decided that you will showcase your research in a book.

Finally, you will want to evaluate not only your final product, but your research process as well. Peer evaluation is a helpful tool in getting a different perspective on your research and your product. Before you even start researching, create a quality checklist for your final product. This will give you working guidelines as you begin to uncover who are the most influential Americans.

Sincerely,

Susie B. Student

APPENDIX B1

GROUPING PLAN CHART

GROUP A	GROUP B	GROUP C

About the Authors

Tracy C. Missett, Ph.D., is an assistant professor at the University of Montana Phyllis J. Washington College of Education and Human Sciences, where she holds the Suzanne and Dave Peterson Endowed Professorship in Gifted Education. Dr. Missett received her Ph.D. and B.A. from the University of Virginia, her J.D. from the University of California, Hastings College of the Law, and her M.A. from Teachers College, Columbia University. While a doctoral student at the University of Virginia, Dr. Missett was a Graduate Research Assistant on a project of the National Research Center on the Gifted and Talented (NRC/GT) and engaged in research on the effectiveness of the CLEAR Curriculum Model. Dr. Missett has published multiple articles and book chapters on topics in gifted education, and she has received awards in both curriculum and research from the National Association for Gifted Children.

Amy Price Azano, Ph.D., is an assistant professor of adolescent literacy at Virginia Tech where her research focuses on rural gifted education, place-based pedagogy, and the literacy needs of rural youth. Dr. Azano teaches graduate level literacy courses to preservice teachers and doctoral students and serves as coprincipal investigator on a 5-year, Jacob K. Javits Department of Education grant seeking to improve gifted education for rural learners. She is also an affiliate faculty member, leading the education research core, with the Virginia Tech Center for Autism Research, and does extensive community outreach in the field of autism. Prior to her current position, Dr. Azano was a researcher and project manager on the "What Works in Gifted Education" study at the National Research Center on the Gifted and Talented (NRC/GT) at the University of Virginia (UVA). Before earning her Ph.D. in English Education from UVA, Dr. Azano taught high school English and served as codirector of UVA's National Writing Project site. Her recent publications can be found in *American Educational Research Journal, English Education, Journal of Advanced Academics, Journal of Research in Rural Education, Journal of Teaching Writing,* and *Teaching Exceptional Children.*

Carolyn M. Callahan, Ph.D., Commonwealth Professor of Education at the University of Virginia, developed and leads the master's and doctoral programs in gifted education, teaches classes in gifted education, and developed the summer and Saturday enrichment programs at UVA. For 20 years, she has been the principal investigator on projects of the National Research Center on the Gifted and Talented (NRC/GT), and she has been principal investigator on five Javits grants. Her work with the NRC/GT and with the Javits projects has focused on curriculum development and implementation. As part of her work with the NRC/GT she was coevaluator for the U.S. Department of Education of the Javits program and conducted a national survey of gifted and talented programs. She has conducted evaluations of grant projects including several Javits grants, state-level programs (e.g., the Advanced Placement initiative in Maine), and local-level gifted programs large and small. She has been recognized as Outstanding Professor of the Commonwealth of Virginia and Distinguished Scholar of the National Association for Gifted Children (NAGC). She has served as president of NAGC and the Association for the Gifted, and as editor of *Gifted Child Quarterly.* Dr. Callahan has published more than 200 articles and 50 book chapters on topics in gifted education with one of those publications considered the definitive book on evaluation. She is the coeditor of the recently published books, *Fundamentals of Gifted Education: Considering Multiple Perspectives* and *Critical Issues in Gifted Education.*

Common Core State Standards Alignment

Domain	Grade 5 ELA-Literacy Common Core State Standards
Writing	L.W.5.1: Write opinion pieces on topics or texts, supporting a point of view with reasons and information. Write opinion pieces on topics or texts, supporting a point of view with reasons and information.
	L.W.5.2: Write informative/explanatory texts to examine a topic and convey ideas and information clearly.
	L.W.5.4: Produce clear and coherent writing in which the development and organization are appropriate to task, purpose, and audience.
	L.W.5.7: Conduct short research projects that use several sources to build knowledge through investigation of different aspects of a topic.
	L.W.5.8: Recall relevant information from experiences or gather relevant information from print and digital sources; summarize or paraphrase information in notes and finished work, and provide a list of sources.
	L.W.5.9: Draw evidence from literary or informational texts to support analysis, reflection, and research.
Speaking and Listening	L.SL.5.1: Engage effectively in a range of collaborative discussions (one-on-one, in groups, and teacher-led) with diverse partners on grade 5 topics and texts, building on others' ideas and expressing their own clearly.
	L.SL.5.2: Summarize a written text read aloud or information presented in diverse media and formats, including visually, quantitatively, and orally.

Domain	Grade 5 ELA-Literacy Common Core State Standards
Speaking and Listening, ***continued***	L.SL.5.3: Summarize the points a speaker makes and explain how each claim is supported by reasons and evidence.
	L.SL.5.4: Report on a topic or text or present an opinion, sequencing ideas logically and using appropriate facts and relevant, descriptive details to support main ideas or themes; speak clearly at an understandable pace.
Reading: Informational Text	L: Quote accurately from a text when explaining what the text says explicitly and when drawing inferences from the text.
	L: Analyze multiple accounts of the same event or topic, noting important similarities and differences in the point of view they represent.
	L.RI.5.7: Draw on information from multiple print or digital sources, demonstrating the ability to locate an answer to a question quickly or to solve a problem efficiently.
	L.RI.5.8: Explain how an author uses reasons and evidence to support particular points in a text, identifying which reasons and evidence support which point(s).
	L.RI.5.9: Integrate information from several texts on the same topic in order to write or speak about the subject knowledgeably.
	L.RI.5.10: By the end of the year, read and comprehend informational texts, including history/social studies, science, and technical texts, at the high end of the grades 4-5 text complexity band independently and proficiently.